WEAPON

THE BROWNING HIGH-POWER PISTOL

LEROY THOMPSON

Series Editor Martin Pegler
Illustrated by Adam Hook & Alan Gilliland

OSPREY PUBLISHING
Bloomsbury Publishing Plc

Kemp House, Chawley Park, Oxford OX2 9PH, UK
29 Earlsfort Terrace, Dublin 2, Ireland
1385 Broadway, 5th Floor, New York, NY 10018, USA
Email: info@ospreypublishing.com
www.ospreypublishing.com

OSPREY is a trademark of Osprey Publishing Ltd

First published in Great Britain in 2020
Transferred to digital print in 2023

A catalogue record for this book is available from the
British Library.

Print ISBN: 978 1 4728 3809 4
ePub: 978 1 4728 3810 0
ePDF: 978 1 4728 3808 7
XML: 978 1 4728 3807 0

Index by Rob Munro
Typeset by PDQ Digital Media Solutions, Bungay, UK
Printed and bound in India by Replika Press Private Ltd.

23 24 25 26 27   10 9 8 7 6 5 4 3 2

The Woodland Trust
Osprey Publishing supports the Woodland Trust, the UK's
leading woodland conservation charity.

www.ospreypublishing.com
To find out more about our authors and books visit our
website. Here you will find extracts, author interviews, details of
forthcoming events and the option to sign-up for our newsletter.

A note on terminology

Because there are so many designations used for the Browning
High-Power, it is necessary to give an explanation of how some
of those designations will be used in this work. First, the term
'High-Power' refers to any pistol marked 'Fabrique Nationale'.
The term 'Hi-Power' refers to those pistols marked 'Browning
Arms Company'. Other terms may be used to apply to the
military FN production High-Powers, including GP (*Grande
Puissance*), GP 35 or P 35. Canadian-produced pistols will
normally be referred to as Inglis High-Powers. British and British
Commonwealth High-Powers will be referred to as the 'L9A1'.
Other military High-Powers may be referred to by the
designation used in their country of use. High-Powers
manufactured under licence are referred to by the designation
used by their manufacturer.

Dedication

In memory of Ed Seyffert: US Navy veteran, career law-
enforcement officer, avid shooter and good friend. Also in
memory of René Smeets, a modern Renaissance man who loved
literature, theatre, history, martial arts and firearms history, as
well as good fellowship with his friends. He edited Belgium's
foremost arms magazine *AMI* (later *FIRE*) for many years and
co-authored a book on combat handguns with me that was far
better for having both the American and European view of
fighting handguns. By knowing René with his contacts at FN, my
knowledge of the FN High-Power, the subject of this work, was
enhanced. I was saddened to learn of his death shortly after I
submitted the material for this book to the publisher. I will
always treasure the hours I spent with René and his wife
Jacqueline. I will miss him greatly.

Acknowledgements

I would like to thank the following who offered their assistance
in the preparation of this work: Tom Knox; Tom Knox Jr.; John
Miller; T.J. Mullin; Wayne Novak; Pete Polizzi; Rock Island
Auction Company; Robert Taubert; Blake Stevens/Collector
Grade Publications; Anthony Vanderlinden.

Editor's note

All images not otherwise credited are from the author's
collection. Metric measurements are used in this book. The
exception is weapons calibre, where imperial is used in many
cases, depending on the context. For ease of comparison please
refer to the following conversion table:

1km = 0.62 miles
1m = 1.09yd / 3.28ft
1cm = 0.39in
1mm = 0.04in
1kg = 2.20lb / 35.27oz

Front cover, above: An early Belgian military High-Power with
tangent sights and slot for the slat-type shoulder stock adopted
for issuance to NCOs and some other troops. (Author's
Collection)
Front cover, below: A British Army soldier firing an L9A1 on the
range at Basra, Iraq, in July 2006. (Photo: Harland Quarrington/
MOD)
Title-page photograph: British Paras on exercise in England; the
officer at left is armed with an Inglis No. 2 Mk 1* High-Power
while the radioman is armed with a Mk 4 (L2A3) Sterling
submachine gun. (© IWM R 16362)

Artist's note

Readers may care to note that the original paintings from which
the colour plates in this book were prepared are available for
private sale. All reproduction copyright whatsoever is retained by
the publishers. All enquiries should be addressed to:

Scorpio, 158 Mill Road, Hailsham, East Sussex BN27 2SH, UK
Email: scorpiopaintings@btinternet.com

The publishers regret that they can enter into no correspondence
upon this matter.

CONTENTS

BROWNING ARMS COMPANY MORGAN UTAH & MONTREAL P.Q.
MADE IN BELGIUM

INTRODUCTION

After 1945, the FN High-Power Pistol ranked as the world's most widely used military handgun, and remains one of the most iconic combat pistols of all time. More than 90 countries have issued the High-Power to military forces or law-enforcement agencies and it has seen use in conflicts from World War II through to the 'War on Terror'.

Chambered for the 9mm Luger (9×19mm) cartridge, which became the world standard during the years after World War II, the High-Power offered the largest magazine capacity of any production handgun (13 rounds) during its first decades and even today offers a capacity close to that of contemporary military pistols. Designed by John Browning, the High-Power improved on the classic Colt M1911 design, especially in its use of a far simpler takedown system. Accurate and reliable, the High-Power was considered the world standard for a semi-automatic combat pistol for a half-century.

The impetus for the design of the High-Power was a French military requirement for a new pistol, the first trials being in 1922. Two French names for the pistol were used: *Grand Rendement* (High Efficiency) and *Grande Puissance* (High Power). Note that models distributed by Browning in the US would be called the 'Hi-Power', while throughout most of the world the pistol was known as the 'High-Power'.

John Browning, who was commissioned to design the pistol, built a pair of prototypes – one locked breech and one blowback – for which a patent was granted in 1927. Both designs incorporated a high-capacity magazine designed by Dieudonné Saive that staggered the cartridges for higher capacity without unduly increasing the grip size. The locked-breech design with a 16-round magazine was the one carried forward for testing. When the Colt M1911 patents expired in 1928, Saive incorporated some aspects of the M1911 design into the *Grand Rendement*. By 1931, the magazine had been shortened to accommodate 13 rounds, the back strap had been curved for a better grip, and the barrel bushing was part of the

slide rather than separate as on the M1911. France did not adopt the pistol, but the Belgian Army did in 1935 as the P 35, a designation by which the pistol is still widely known. During its long production – more than 80 years – the design has evolved slightly, but a current-production High-Power is still easily recognizable as a descendent of the original P 35.

Pre-World War II users of the High-Power included Argentina, Belgium, Estonia, Lithuania and Paraguay. After conquering Belgium in May 1940, Germany went on to make use of FN's manufacturing plant to produce more than 300,000 High-Powers for use by the Waffen-SS, *Fallschirmjäger* (airborne troops) and others. The High-Power as produced by Inglis in Canada also saw usage with the Canadian, British and other Commonwealth armed forces during World War II. Inglis also produced the High-Power for the Chiang Kai-shek regime in China.

In the years after World War II, the High-Power became standard for most NATO armed forces as well as scores of others throughout the world, though many have subsequently replaced it with newer pistols such as the SIG Sauer P226, Glock 17 or FN Five-seveN.

DEVELOPMENT
Towards the High-Power

THE M1900

To trace the development of the Browning High-Power it is important to understand the relationship between John Browning and Browning Arms Company of the USA and Fabrique Nationale (FN) of Belgium. Browning had begun experimenting with self-loading weapons in 1889, resulting in the M1895 machine gun. He also demonstrated his first semi-automatic pistol design, a gas-operated .38-calibre weapon, in 1895. In 1896, Browning gave Colt the rights to distribute this pistol and other pistols on which he was working in the USA.

The original FN/Browning semi-automatic pistol, the M1900, a John Browning design for FN c.1896. The M1900 is noteworthy as being the first production semi-automatic pistol to use a slide. More than 700,000 would eventually be built. (Courtesy of Rock Island Auction Company)

At this point Browning did not have a European distributor for his pistols, but he did have a pistol he thought would appeal to the European market. Chambered for a 7.65×17mm cartridge that would come to be known as the 7.65mm Browning, or in Colt pistols as the .32 ACP (Automatic Colt Pistol), the pistol was a blowback design. Patent papers were filed in the USA in December 1897, with the patent being granted in March 1899. Colt was not interested in a pocket semi-automatic pistol at that time, however. Browning found his European distributor in FN, which signed an agreement with Browning in July 1897 to distribute his semi-automatic pistol designs. Browning would maintain a close relationship with FN until his death in 1926 (Ezell 1981: 207).

The first 3,900 examples of the Browning-designed 7.65mm pistol were produced during 1899. In 1900, Belgium adopted the pistol with some slight modifications, which simplified production, for issuance to Belgian Army officers as the M1900. Initially, 20,000 M1900s were ordered. By the time production of the M1900 ceased in 1910/11, a total of 724,500 had been produced for military and commercial sales (Ezell 1981: 211).

THE M1903

In 1902, Browning made his first visit to FN in Liége, primarily to promote his self-loading shotgun, the Auto-5, which FN licensed for production; he spent three months assisting FN in setting up production of the self-loading shotgun. Browning also brought along a prototype of an improved self-loading pistol chambered for the more powerful 9×20mm cartridge. The pistol, which went into production as the M1903,

A Husqvarna m/1907 pistol from the collections of the Swedish Air Force Museum. The bulk of M1903s were actually produced under licence in Sweden by Husqvarna as the m/1907. After initial adoption, Sweden ordered around 10,000 M1903 pistols from FN. Sweden began domestic production in 1917. Although there is speculation that difficulty in procuring the pistols during World War I was the impetus for Sweden to begin domestic production of the m/1907, this is not clear (Vanderlinden 2013: 183). Total Swedish production of the m/1907 was 94,731, with only 6,145 of that number for commercial sales (Ezell 1981: 211). (Wikimedia/Swedish Air Force Museum/ CC BY 4.0)

The m/1907 was the standard sidearm of the Swedish armed forces until 1940, when it was replaced by the Lahti L-35. This M1903 was used by Gösta Benckert, a Swedish officer in the Swedish Volunteer Corps, during the Winter War in Finland (1939–40). (Wikimedia/Swedish Army Museum/CC BY 4.0)

was intended primarily for military sales. Unlike the M1900 that used a striker, the M1903 had an exposed hammer. In 1907, FN began production of the M1903, which continued in production until 1927, with a hiatus during World War I. A total of 58,442 were produced, with Belgium, Czechoslovakia, the Netherlands, Paraguay, Russia, Sweden and Turkey adopting it (Vanderlinden 2013: 178–80).

THE M1910

The next John Browning/FN project was the M1910, used by the Belgian armed forces between 1919 and 1933, as production of the M1900 had been discontinued. Thousands of M1910s were sold to Japan between 1937 and

Chambered in either 7.65mm (.32 ACP) or 9mm Browning (.380 ACP), the M1910 was a simplified, more compact design that proved extremely popular as a civilian and police pistol, with a limited number of military sales. An FN M1910 may be one of the most notorious pistols in history, as one was used by Gavrilo Princip to assassinate Archduke Franz Ferdinand of Austria on 28 June 1914, an act that precipitated the start of World War I. Pistols of this model were also used to kill Paul Doumer, the President of France, on 7 May 1932, and to assassinate Huey Long, Governor of Louisiana, on 10 September 1935. (Wikimedia/Askild Antonsen/CC BY 2.0)

1940, the pistol being popular with Japanese officers who purchased their own personal weapons (Vanderlinden 2013: 229). With the exception of breaks in production between 1914 and 1919, in 1940 and in the mid-1950s, the M1910 was produced from 1910 to 1975. The design was copied in Czechoslovakia, Finland and Germany. Total M1910 production had reached 460,000 by the time of the German invasion of Belgium in May 1940. (The Germans did not produce the M1910 during their occupation of Belgium, but did complete over 6,000 pistols of other types after capturing the FN plant.) Based on serial numbers, approximately 285,000 M1910 pistols were produced after World War II (Vanderlinden 2013: 212–13).

The M1910/22 proved appealing to military and police purchasers, with versions in both 7.65×17mm and 9×17mm. After the German occupation of Belgium in May 1940, 363,200 M1910/22 pistols were produced at FN's plant for the German armed forces. M1910/22 production for police and civilian orders, with perhaps small military orders, continued after World War II, with more than 760,000 of the model being manufactured before production ceased in the 1960s (Ezell 1981: 215). (© Royal Armouries XII.3627)

THE M1910/22

A widely encountered variant of the M1910 is the M1910/22. A February 1923 order from Yugoslavia called for a barrel length of 114mm rather than the standard M1910 barrel length of 89mm, reportedly to increase accuracy, and an eight-round 7.65×17mm/seven-round 9×17mm magazine rather than the standard M1910 capacity of 7/6 rounds. For the Yugoslav order, 9×17mm pistols were produced. Because the order was for 60,000 pistols, FN willingly altered the M1910 by installing the longer barrel and extending the slide by adding a sheet-metal cap with a front sight installed. The frame was extended to take the higher-capacity magazine. The order was especially lucrative for FN, as Yugoslavia also ordered Mauser rifles and ammunition for the pistols and rifles (Vanderlinden 2013: 239).

DESIGNING THE HIGH-POWER

It should be pointed out that designating the High-Power as an 'improvement' on the M1911 may be an oversimplification. Browning was constrained by his own patents for the Colt M1911, the patents for which had been sold to Colt. Incorporating exact copies of elements of the M1911's design in the High-Power would have infringed those patents.

Design of the High-Power was also dictated to some extent by the requirements of a potential customer – the French Government. Although France had purchased some Colt M1911s during World

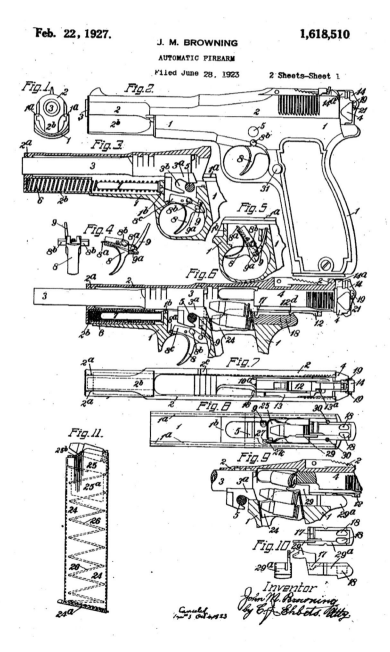

John Browning's original patent drawings for what would become the High-Power. (US Patent Office)

THE COLT M1911 AND ITS INFLUENCE

As the M1910 was entering production, John Browning had been involved in the design and military trials of arguably his most famous pistol – the Colt M1911. Prior to his work on what would become the M1911, which served as the primary US service pistol for 74 years and saw limited US military use for a century, Browning had designed other pistols that had been tested for US military adoption, including the Colt M1900 .38 Auto. An improved model, the M1902 .38 Auto, was also tested. Based at least partially on experiences facing fanatical Moro attackers during the Philippine Insurrection (1899–1902), the USA expressed a desire for a .45-calibre semi-automatic pistol. Browning's first design, the M1905 Military Model in .45 ACP calibre, appeared on the market in April 1906 (Thompson 2011: 10).

The M1905 .45 pistol was tested at the Royal Small Arms Factory at Enfield in the UK, but was not adopted. In the USA, Frankford Arsenal along with Union Metallic Cartridge Company worked on developing a .45-calibre service cartridge, resulting in the 'Cal. .45 Automatic Pistol Ball Cartridge, Model of 1911' firing a 230-grain (14.90g) bullet at 259m/sec. Extensive trials of semi-automatic pistol designs resulted in the US adoption of the Browning-designed Colt M1911 pistol, with the first US Government orders placed on 21 April 1911 (Thompson 2011: 15). Unlike other Browning designs, FN did not market a version of the Colt M1911 for the European market, though a substantial number would later be purchased from Colt for British service in World War I.

Some comments on the design and operating system of the Colt M1911 are important because they had an influence on the later design of the Browning/FN High-Power Pistol. The Colt M1911 features a locked breech employing downward displacement of the barrel via a pivoting link at its rear, which is unlocked after the barrel and slide travel rearward together during recoil, at which point the slide continues to travel rearward, ejecting the spent case and chambering a new cartridge. This link is held in place by the slide stop, which also holds open the slide after the last round is fired. A forked barrel bushing located at the front of the slide holds the recoil spring in place by retaining a knurled tube. A tubular guide rod at the rear of the spring holds the spring in place. Both a thumb safety and a grip safety are incorporated (Wilson & Hogg 1975: 193–94).

Disassembly of the M1911 is a relatively complicated operation, as the barrel bushing must be rotated while applying downward pressure on the knurled tube retaining the recoil spring. Care must be taken that the recoil spring does not pop out against spring tension. Then, the slide must be retracted so that the slide stop may be pushed free. This allows the barrel slide group to be pushed forward off the receiver. After the barrel, recoil spring and recoil-spring guide rod have been removed, the pistol is ready for maintenance. As can be appreciated, this process exposes a pistol being cleaned in the field to loss of various small parts: a disadvantage in a military pistol and an issue that would be addressed in the High-Power.

John Browning's M1911 pistol, adopted by the US armed forces and used for a century, is shown here with the cavalry drop holster. (Author's Collection)

MANUFACTURE D'ARMES DE PARIS

A right-side view of one of the original 1933 French trials pistols. This design was a marked departure from the *Grand Rendement* (High Efficiency) pistol as it utilized a single-stack magazine and was chambered for the 7.65×20mm Longue cartridge. As the pistol did not use the 9×19mm cartridge, the Browning locked-breech design was replaced with a blowback design. (Author's Collection)

War I, by May 1921, French military armament specialists had expressed interest in a powerful military semi-automatic pistol in 9mm calibre; it had to have a 20cm barrel, a magazine capacity of at least 15 rounds, weigh 1kg or less, have a graduated rear sight adjustable to 600m and be capable of mounting a stock (Stevens 1984: 13).

The French contacted FN about a pistol that would meet these specifications. When John Browning was approached about designing such a pistol, he responded that he did see a need for a magazine capacity of more than seven or eight rounds. As a result, Dieudonné Saive of FN undertook a study of the feasibility of constructing a pistol that met the French specifications. His first step was the development of a double-column magazine that held 15 cartridges. This prototype magazine was presented to Browning, who took it back to the USA for further study (Stevens 1984: 13–14).

Working with his brother Edward, Browning produced two prototype pistols that would use a 15-round magazine. One design used a barrel that would recoil but was not locked to the slide (basically a blowback), while the second had a barrel that tilted downward upon recoil to unlock from the slide. This latter design operated in a similar manner to the Colt M1911, but without the barrel link. Because of contractual arrangements with Colt, the two prototypes were demonstrated for Colt, which undertook the patent application on behalf of Browning but were not interested in producing the pistol. As a result, Val Browning, John Browning's son, took the prototypes to FN for demonstration (Stevens 1984: 14).

In the patent application of 28 June 1923 (John Browning's last; he died on 26 November 1926 aged 71), it is noted that the design was such that various parts performed multiple functions, thus simplifying the design and making the pistol easier to disassemble. It is worth noting that Colt's patent attorney had informed Browning that the double-column magazine was not patentable and, therefore, details about the magazine should not be included that might help competitors (Stevens 1984: 22). The design incorporated a connecting bar for the trigger and sear that prevented the pistol from firing unless the slide was locked in the forward position. The improved locking system for the barrel/slide was stronger and enhanced accuracy by allowing the barrel to move rearward in linear fashion (Ezell 1981: 221–22).

THE M1923 AND M1928

Val Browning lived in Liége and so he was involved in the development of what became the M1922, based on his father's design. Prototypes of the pistol were demonstrated to a French trials board and performed well, though the trials board did request that the pistol have an external hammer and be lighter in weight. Rather than send prototypes back and forth across the Atlantic, Saive designed the changes requested by the trials board, resulting in what was designated the M1923. This pistol was entered in French trials conducted in March 1925. Once again, changes were requested, primarily to reduce the weight further. The trials board also stated that they considered the pistol to be too complex for easy maintenance in the field (Vanderlinden 2013: 289). One important feature of the High-Power arose from another French contract: an order for M1922 pistols for use by France's Marine nationale (navy), for which FN developed a finish using a phosphate base with black enamel paint over it. This corrosion-resistant finish was not only later used on the High-Power, but also the FN FAL battle rifle and the FNC assault rifle (Vanderlinden 2015a).

As the pistol evolved, the 15-round magazine was discarded in favour of a 13-round magazine, thus shortening the grip and reducing overall weight. The tangent sights that had been used on earlier models were also eliminated. After the death of John Browning, Saive supervised the incorporation of modifications in the pistol. Continuing French trials resulted in evolving specifications and the pistol became known as the *Grand Rendement* (High Efficiency). By 1927/28, it had begun to resemble what would become known as the GP (*Grande Puissance*; High Power) (Vanderlinden 2013: 291).

An important aspect of the GP was that the patent on the Colt M1911 had run out in 1928, thus allowing Saive to incorporate some of its features into the GP. These consisted primarily of a rebounding firing pin and a stationary, rather than a removable, breech bolt. Out of respect for his long relationship with FN, however, John Browning's surname was retained on what became known as the Browning M1928 (Stevens 1984: 37). Note that the designation 'Browning-Saive High-Power' is sometimes used.

Oval ejection port used on *Grand Rendement* pistols built before adoption as the GP 35. (Author's Collection)

REFINING THE HIGH-POWER

By 1929, and despite the lack of a French contract, FN had decided to market the GP for military sales. FN's policy was to delay the start of production until a substantial military contract had been received, however, and it was deemed that size, calibre (9×19mm) and price did not in themselves make the GP a viable commercial product. Marketing of the GP became more difficult after the Stock Market Crash of 1929. It also became apparent that a major French order would not materialize (Vanderlinden 2013: 291). Nevertheless, Saive continued to work on designs for ongoing French trials, including a model of 1936 that incorporated the High-Power's locked breech (Stevens 1984: 45). To give an idea of the effect of the Great Depression on FN: in June 1929, FN had 9,138 employees, a number that would decline to 2,580 by May 1934. Saive continued to improve the design of the GP, however, by 1931 incorporating the curved back strap and fixed barrel bushing. At this point, the GP closely resembled the Browning High-Power in the form in which it would appear as the world's most popular military pistol (Stevens 1984: 39).

By 1934, two versions of the High-Power were ready for sale – one with a 1,000m tangent rear sight and the other with a fixed rear sight (Stevens 1984: 53). Owing to the agreement between Colt and FN, which divided the world into sales territories, the High-Power was not marketed in the USA upon its introduction. In fact, prior to World War II, the only two High-Powers reported to be in the USA were one residing in the Colt collection and another in the hands of Val Browning. With European countries arming for the impending conflict, however, there appeared to be a large potential market for what was arguably the world's most advanced military pistol (Stevens 1984: 60).

Based on FN's long experience of military contracts requiring special features on the pistols ordered, Saive had designed the High-Power so that small changes (lanyard ring, special sights, etc.) could be made at minimal costs (Vanderlinden 2013: 291). A good example of FN's prescience arose with the first Belgian military order of 1,000 pistols for field-testing. These trials pistols are often known as 'oval port' models because of the shape of their ejection ports, but they were still considered to be the *Grand Rendement* design. After acceptance by the Belgian purchasing

BELOW LEFT
The tangent rear sight given to some pre-World War II Belgian military GP 35 pistols. (Author's Collection)

BELOW RIGHT
The fixed rear sight given to some pre-World War II Belgian military GP 35 pistols. (Courtesy of Rock Island Auction Company)

THE HIGH-POWER EXPOSED

9×19mm Browning GP 35

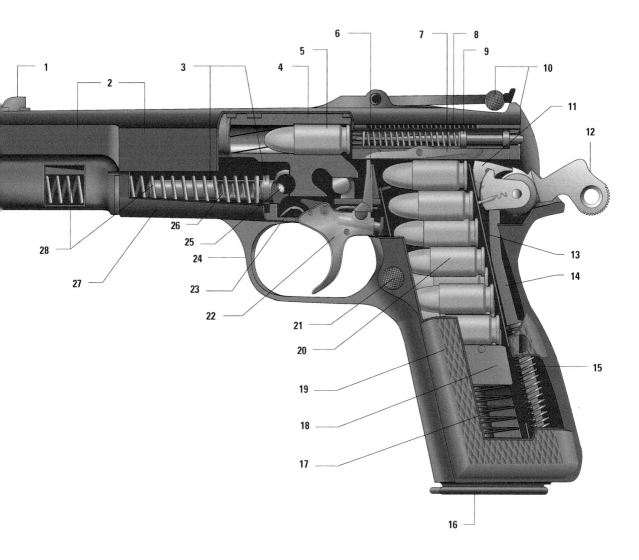

1. Front sight
2. Slide
3. Recoil-spring guide
4. Barrel
5. Cartridge in chamber
6. Trigger lever
7. Sear lever
8. Firing-pin spring
9. Firing pin
10. Rear sights

11. Sear
12. Hammer
13. Sear spring
14. Hammer strut
15. Hammer spring
16. Magazine base plate
17. Magazine spring
18. Magazine follower
19. Grip
20. Cartridges in magazine

21. Magazine catch
22. Trigger
23. Trigger spring
24. Trigger guard
25. Detent ball
26. Detent ball spring
27. Receiver
28. Recoil spring

A pre-World War II High-Power disassembled into its primary component parts. From top: slide, barrel, recoil spring and spring guide rod, frame; magazine at left, slide release/takedown at right. Note the pre-war cam slot on the barrel. (Author's Collection)

commission the pistols were designated *Grande Puissance* (GP), and changes were requested in the hammer design and the method for ejection of spent cartridge cases. Also requested was a system to keep the magazine from dropping free when the magazine-release button was pressed – a measure intended to keep magazines from being lost, as their cost was considered high (Vanderlinden 2013: 291).

While Belgium's adoption of the GP was a boon for FN, it became apparent that France would not adopt a foreign pistol design. Though FN attempted the ploy of marking pistols supplied for French trials with 'MANUFACTURE D'ARMES DE PARIS', FN's French affiliate, France, in fact, adopted the M1935 pistol in 7.65×20mm Longue calibre (Vanderlinden 2013: 292).

Few modifications were made to the design of the GP from its introduction until World War II, though one important change was made in the late 1930s. It was discovered that the semi-circular cam cut in the barrel lug could cause metal fatigue in the forward portion of the lug, eventually leading to a fracture at the thinnest portion of the lug after thousands of rounds had been fired. A simple machining modification cut a more squared-off contour of the cam cut, reducing the effect of slamming down as it unlocked in recoil (Stevens 1984: 70). It is possible that the change in cam cuts may have originated with a customer request, though this is not clear.

THE SHOULDER STOCK

One result of the Belgian military trials was the adoption of a shoulder stock, holster and magazine pouch to accompany the pistol. Various types of shoulder stocks had already been tested for demonstration during the French trials, including metal collapsible skeleton stocks. The version accepted by the Belgian armed forces was a detachable wooden stock of slat type that attached to a leather holster. Many other countries adopted versions in which the holster was attached to the stock. These stocks were intended for use with tangent-sighted High-Power pistols, having a slot on the rear of the grip (Vanderlinden 2013: 294–95). There were actually two types of tangent sights, both with graduations from 50m to 500m. However, one type had the markings compacted to only fill about 60 per cent of the sight leaf, while the other version filled the entire sight leaf. The first type of sight was intended for pistols with shoulder stocks issued to NCOs and other troops, while the second type was on pistols without shoulder stocks issued to officers during 1939–40 (Vanderlinden 2013: 297–98). Issuance of stocked GP pistols was based on the assumption that they could replace the carbine with NCOs and other personnel not issued a rifle. Only a limited number of pre-war High-Powers had fixed sights and are readily identifiable by the presence of the shoulder-stock slot (Vanderlinden 2015a).

Pre-World War II Belgian military High-Power with its shoulder stock affixed; these pistols were intended for Belgian enlisted personnel who would not normally be issued a rifle. (Courtesy of Rock Island Auction Company)

POST-WAR MODIFICATIONS

When German armed forces invaded Belgium in May 1940, the FN factory fell into enemy hands, and would be used to produce the High-Power – as the P 640(b) – as well as other weapons. This is discussed in the Use chapter, as are the High-Powers produced in Canada by Inglis.

When German armed forces retreated from Belgium in late August and early September 1944, a substantial stockpile of parts was left behind in the FN factory. The last Germans left the factory on 5 September 1944, and within a matter of days, assembly of High-Power pistols resumed. The US 3d Armored Division had liberated Liége and US soldiers, always interested in acquiring handguns, proved willing customers for High-Powers. Pistols initially assembled from parts left over from the German occupation were crude, however. In some cases their parts will not interchange with those of pistols produced before the German occupation. Nevertheless, these pistols, identifiable by an 'A' before the serial number, proved popular with US Army troops who purchased the bulk of production, but some went to British, Free Belgian and Luxembourgeois troops (Vanderlinden 2013: 334).

As production resumed after the war, FN employees had to refurbish and repair the machinery used to produce the High-Power while attempting to generate cash by fabricating pistols (Stevens 1984: 151). FN pistols produced after 1945 incorporated the magazine safety once again (Vanderlinden 2013: 337). In 1947, FN developed a heat-treating process that allowed use of a hardened one-piece slide, instead of the previous design that had required use of a hardened plug staked into place in the breech face (Stevens 1984: 152).

During the 1950s, FN incorporated various changes in the basic High-Power design. In 1950, the change made in the shape of the cam slot in the 1930s was further modified as the cam slot was narrowed and the cam in the frame was altered to be consistent with the new dimensions of the slot. As a result, barrels produced prior to 1950 will fit post-1950 frames but will not normally function reliably or accurately. Shortly after the change to the cam in 1950, another change was made to the magazine safety so it would operate more positively, which required a clearance slot to be milled in the frame to accept the improved magazine safety (Stevens 1984: 161).

NEW DIRECTIONS

Throughout the 1950s FN experimented with other versions of the classic GP. Aware of the trend towards double-action semi-automatic pistols, inspired to a large extent by the experience with German designs such as the Walther PP/PPK and P 38, which had been encountered in substantial quantities by Allied troops during World War II, Saive was assigned the task of designing a double-action version of the P 640(b). During this same period, and probably influenced by Colt's introduction of the alloy-framed Commander pistol in 1950, Saive experimented with an alloy-framed GP. Though both innovations showed promise, GPs were selling well in the traditional format so the designs did not proceed to production. FN would re-visit both later, however. Saive retired from FN in November 1954 to be succeeded by Ernest Vervier.

During 1958, a change was made to the GP's sear that reduced the initial slack in the trigger pull (Stevens 1984: 167). In 1962, a working group within FN was tasked with studying the GP to identify design improvements and cost-saving measures. Among the modifications incorporated was an improved and more reliable extractor that was mounted externally (Stevens 1984: 168). As another cost-saving measure, the 'disassembly notch' (also known as the 'half-moon cut' or 'thumb print') on the slide was eliminated. Production costs were lowered and manufacture made easier when FN changed from machining each barrel from a forged billet to precisely cutting the barrel from rifled tubing, then brazing to it a rear section that incorporated the barrel lug and cocking cam slot (Stevens 1984: 169). During 1962–63, the rust blue finish that had previously been used on the HP was replaced with salt blueing, aluminium magazine followers were replaced by plastic ones and high-impact, Cycolac AMS (alphamethyl styrene) synthetic grips were introduced (Vanderlinden 2013: 350).

A good view of the half-moon cut on a West German Police High-Power. (Author's Collection)

A pistol showing the standardized FN features on military pistols as of 1965, including black Cycolac AMS grips, Parkerized or varnished finish and a lanyard ring. (Author's Collection)

FN strove for standardization of the GP during the 1960s. As of 1965, the standard GP pistol supplied for military contracts incorporated the following features: black Cycolac AMS grips; a pivoting, visible extractor; a rectangular front sight; a U-notch rear sight; a lanyard ring; a Parkerized and varnished finish; and a Parkerized barrel (Stevens 1984: 173). Stevens observes that, though FN had standardized the GP, the availability of various earlier examples in some armouries caused difficulties with parts interchangeability. He notes, for example, that the Dutch Army had a total of 72,000 GP pistols of five different types. These consisted of 12,000 Inglis High-Powers, with the remainder representing four types of post-war FN production, designated (based on the contract years) as 1947, 1949, 1955 or 1967. Among the difficulties that arose with interchangeability was the fact that the 1947-model GPs had the early post-war larger receiver and cam dimensions, while the later FN GPs did not. Front sights were attached in a different manner among the versions and there were two types of extractors (Stevens 1984: 176).

BELOW LEFT
The classic High-Power ring hammer. (Author's Collection)

BELOW RIGHT
The later High-Power spur hammer. (Author's Collection)

A High-Power with adjustable sights; these aided accuracy but could catch on a jacket lining during the draw. (Author's Collection)

By 1969/70 FN had automated the process for polishing and blueing the GP. The blueing process was now designated electrolyte blueing. A change that was liked by some GP users and disliked by others took place in 1972 when the traditional ring hammer was replaced by a spur hammer (Vanderlinden 2013: 350). Traditionalists liked the ring hammer, as those who carried the pistol concealed felt it was less likely to snag during the draw. Conversely, some GP users liked the spur hammer because it made thumb-cocking the pistol easier.

In 1972, FN started offering an adjustable rear sight with a higher front sight as an option (Vanderlinden 2013: 350). Although the adjustable rear sight made the High-Power easier to zero for use with varying types of ammunition, once again it made the pistol more likely to snag when drawing from concealment.

THREE NEW MODELS

FN changed its name in 1973 from Fabrique Nationale d'Armes de Guerre to Fabrique Nationale Herstal, reflecting the more diversified endeavours of the company. The latter title is used to this day and is often abbreviated to 'FNH'. In addition to the version of the GP with the adjustable rear sight, FNH offered two 'standard' versions of the GP: the traditional, fixed-sight version designated 'Vigilante' and the tangent-sight version designated 'Capitan'. The following options were offered

BROWNING ARMS HI-POWERS IN THE US MARKET

Versions of the GP designated for the US market through Browning Arms Company were introduced during 1954 (Eger 2018). These included standard military-style pistols marked 'Browning Arms Company' and designated as the 'Hi-Power'. A handsome Hi-Power was the engraved Browning Renaissance Model, though pistols with similar engraving were also marketed under FN markings. As of 1958, Browning Arms expanded into Canada, with Montreal serving as the distribution centre along with St. Louis, Missouri, in the USA. Both 'ST. LOUIS, MO & MONTREAL P.Q.' were henceforth included on the Browning Hi-Power slide legend (Stevens 1984: 219–20).

An interesting marketing decision resulted in the introduction in 1954 of the three-gun set of Browning semi-automatics, in regular blue and Renaissance engraved versions. Each boxed set consisted of a Hi-Power, a .380 ACP M1910 and a .25 ACP Baby Browning. In the USA, firearms collectors purchased Renaissance sets, but the standard-version sets were also purchased to offer options for carrying. The Hi-Power could be carried as a holster pistol firing the service 9×19mm cartridge; the M1910 could be carried as a pocket or concealment pistol by a male or female member of the family; and the Baby Browning could be carried as a waistcoat-pocket or purse pistol. Although Renaissance sets were not shot by many owners, others – realizing that the pistols could be shot as readily as the standard blued models – shot and carried their Renaissance Hi-Powers. One friend of the author had an ambidextrous safety installed on his Renaissance Hi-Power and added Spegel custom grips so that he could carry the Hi-Power as his combat pistol.

An important event from the marketing point of view occurred in 1977 when FN purchased Browning Arms. As a result, FN could now market the GP and its other arms directly in the USA (Stevens 1984: 221).

Renaissance engraved Hi-Power of the type sold by Browning Arms Company in the USA and Canada. (Author's Collection)

for these two pistols: blued finish or phosphate and lacquer finish; and the inclusion of a lanyard ring. Another change around this time was the incorporation of a new muzzle bushing designed to protect the muzzle's crown (Stevens 1984: 177). The extended barrel bushing, which offered protection to the barrel's crown, was introduced in 1973 but was eliminated in 1989 (jaypee 2017).

The alloy-framed version of the GP, which had originally been produced experimentally in the early 1950s, was marketed commercially in the early 1970s as well. With a weight of 700g compared to 900g, the assumption was that the alloy-framed GP would appeal to police officers who had to carry a pistol for long periods. A black anodized finish was used on the alloy-framed GP (Stevens 1984: 177). A member of the Gendarmerie Royale Belgique once told the author that alloy-framed GPs were requested from FNH for use by Belgian motorcycle officers.

In 1973, FNH faced a problem competing with other firearms manufacturers due to the high cost of labour in Belgium. As a result, the company opened a production facility in Viana do Castelo, Portugal. FNH would continue to produce parts, but finishing and assembly would be carried out at Viana using cheaper labour: man-hours in Portugal were one-third the cost in Belgium. Company technicians established a training school to teach engraving, polishing, surface treatment and assembly (Francotte 2008: 386).

In 1975, FNH began work on a pistol designed for target shooting in matches. Designated the 'Competition' model, this variant had a barrel of 152mm to conform to *Union internationale de tir* (UIT; 'International Shooting Union') standards. An integral counterweight increased the sighting distance to 192mm, well below the UIT maximum. Other modifications included consistent tension of the barrel bushing on the barrel, an adjustable rear sight, a redesigned magazine safety that did not adversely affect trigger pull and a hammer modified for a crisper lighter pull (Stevens 1984: 224–25).

THE MARK II

In 1982, the Mark II version of the High-Power was introduced, to a great extent to address many of the perceived deficiencies in the High-Power as a combat pistol. Among the Mark II's features were an ambidextrous safety, low-profile sights, ribbed slide, roll pins instead of solid trigger pins and a straight feed ramp for enhanced reliability (Stevens 1984: 183). Early Mark II pistols had forged frames, while later ones had cast frames (Vanderlinden 2013: 351). Custom gunsmiths who worked on High-Powers had incorporated many of these features such as the ambidextrous safety and enhanced feed ramp previously. As an added safety feature the firing-pin safety was introduced in the Mark II *c*.1988, though some sources argue that this feature was introduced for the law-enforcement market on a version designated the MK IIIS in January 1989 (jaypee 2017).

The Competition model of the High-Power made by FNH for a time. (Author's Collection)

7.65×21mm HIGH-POWERS

The late 1970s and early 1980s also saw the introduction of the GP chambered in 7.65×21mm Parabellum (.30 Luger). This was the original chambering for the Luger pistol, though it had long been rendered obsolete by the 9×19mm Parabellum cartridge. However, in various countries civilians were not allowed to own weapons in military calibres. It would appear that only changing the GP's barrel to one chambered for the 7.65×21mm would allow FNH to market the pistol in this calibre (Vanderlinden 2013: 351). However, at least one source states that the slide was lighter, with more material machined away, and that the barrel was of a smaller diameter. The magazines were also reportedly marked for 7.65/.30. Reportedly, however, the pistols will function with standard High-Power 9×19mm magazines (Various 2012). Countries in which 7.65×21mm GPs were reportedly sold included France, Italy and West Germany. As there are other countries that do not allow civilians to own 9×19mm pistols, it is likely that 7.65×21mm GPs were also sold elsewhere. Vanderlinden reports that in the period 1986–89, 1,500 7.65×21mm GPs were imported into the USA through Browning International for sale (Vanderlinden 2013: 351). As most US shooters would have preferred 9×19mm pistols, the 7.65×21mm GPs were mostly sold as curiosities or collector's items.

THE MARK III

The Mark III version of the High-Power was introduced in 1989 and incorporated a passive firing-pin safety. Taking note of the popularity of pistols with a double-action trigger pull, FNH experimented with variations on this system. An interesting Mark III variant employs the SFS (Safety Fast Shooting) action in which, once the chamber is loaded, the hammer is pushed forward to the down position thus applying the safety. To prepare the pistol to fire, the safety is pushed downward, thus bringing the hammer back to the cocked position. The SFS system is intended to eliminate the harder trigger pull for the first shot when using a conventional DA/SA (Double Action/Single Action) pistol. The SFS design, introduced in 1996, was licensed from another Liège-based company, Recherche Developpement-Industrialisation Hubert (Vanderlinden 2013: 351). In the USA, where there is a substantial market for pistols designed for individual self-defence, the SFS version did not prove popular.

FNH also experimented with a more conventional double-action design often designated the 'HP-DA'. This pistol was developed at least partially to compete in the US Joint Service Small Arms Program's XM-9 Pistol Trials that would result in the adoption of the Beretta M9 by US forces in the mid-1980s. An examination of the HP-DA pistol shows that it is obviously based on the

High-Power. The trigger is of DA/SA type, however, and is further forward in the trigger guard when the pistol is de-cocked for a double-action pull. The trigger guard is larger to accommodate the double-action trigger, and there is a de-cocker safety. The pistol was marketed in the USA as the Browning Hi-Power BDA (Browning Double Action). For easier concealment, compact models were also offered. The pistol was discontinued in 1987 but was then redesigned as a double-action-only pistol and re-introduced in 1990. This later version achieved some success in European military and law-enforcement sales (Popenker n.d.). Finland adopted the FNH version, the HP-DA, as its service pistol, designating it the 9.00 PIST 80-91.

FNH's double-action-only version of the High-Power was intended to have more appeal to the law-enforcement market. (Author's Collection)

.40 S&W HIGH-POWERS

During the 1980s, many US law-enforcement agencies adopted .40 S&W pistols to gain enhanced stopping power while retaining the appealing features of many 9×19mm pistols. Although the High-Power was not widely used among US law-enforcement agencies, many civilians who used the pistol were also interested in enhanced stopping power. As a result, FN introduced a High-Power in .40 S&W chambering, with the first examples becoming available in August 1994. All of these pistols used the stronger cast frames, which continued in use from that point for both .40 S&W and 9×19mm High-Powers. Cast frames are readily identifiable by grooves on the base by the magazine well. While the 9×19mm High-Power employs two recoil lugs atop the barrel, the .40 S&W version employs three.

Overall length of the .40 S&W pistol is 6.4mm greater and, because of the thicker slide and barrel, weight is 57g more. The magazine holds ten .40 S&W cartridges; a 'mousetrap' spring ejects the magazine with some force when the magazine-release button is pressed. After only a few .40 S&W High-Powers had been delivered, however, they were recalled due to problems with the chamber specifications, and deliveries did not recommence until December 1994 (Various 1995: 48). Based on the experience of the author and others he knows who have used the .40 S&W High-Power, even users with strong hands find it very difficult to disassemble the pistol because of its heavy recoil spring. Pulling back the slide to chamber a round is also notably more difficult.

The .40 S&W High-Power was built heavier to handle the more powerful cartridge popular among American law-enforcement agencies. The .40 S&W High-Power used a much heavier spring, resulting in the slide being harder to pull back and increasing the difficulty of disassembly. (Author's Collection)

In 2000, Browning Arms halted production of the Hi-Power, though in 2002, the Mark III Practical and Mark III Standard models appeared in the company's catalogue. Production of the Practical model ceased in 2006, while the Standard remained in production through to late 2017 or early 2018 (Eger 2018). As of early February 2018, Browning Arms announced that the Hi-Power would no longer be in production. However, because of the numbers that have been produced, the pistol will remain available throughout the world for many years.

USE
The High-Power goes to war

EARLY ADOPTION

Although the High-Power certainly saw combat with the Belgian Army in 1940, it is possible that it also saw use at an earlier date. Showing creativity in marketing the GP, FN had made it a point to demonstrate the pistol to visiting military officers and government officials, such as a Peruvian delegation that visited Belgium to purchase FN-produced Mauser rifles (Vanderlinden 2013: 292). Note that Peru did recommend purchase of the GP. There was also an order from Paraguay c.1936 and, though the three-year Chaco War between Paraguay and Bolivia had ended in June 1935, it is possible that the High-Power was blooded in skirmishes along the Paraguayan/Bolivian border. Another South American order for 1,600 GPs came from Argentina in 1937 (Vanderlinden 2013: 312).

An Argentine Navy High-Power with shoulder stock affixed. (Author's Collection)

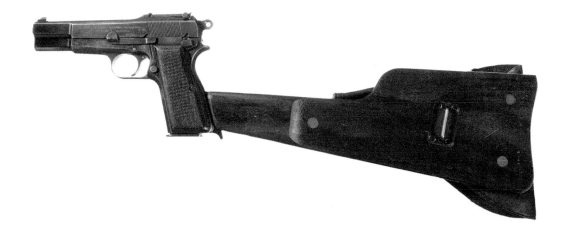

A left-side view of one of the 2,400 Finnish High-Powers shipped from FN during February and March 1940. Some of these pistols were reportedly for the Finnish Air Force, though the Finnish Army received most of them. The stock is of a similar type to those supplied to the Belgian Army. (Author's Collection)

Along with the Belgian military orders, FN also received orders for GPs from China (5,000 slotted and tangent-sighted), Lithuania (*c*.5,000 slotted and tangent-sighted) and Estonia (Stevens 1984: 67–69). Despite not adopting the GP initially, the looming prospect of war led France to order 1,000 of the pistols in September 1939. France was in the process of re-evaluating adoption of the GP shortly before the defeat of that country in May–June 1940.

During the early months of 1940, Sweden and Finland ordered 1,000 and 1,500 High-Power pistols respectively (Stevens 1984: 72). A total of 2,400 High-Powers with shoulder stocks were delivered to Finland, 900 in February 1940 and 1,500 in March 1940. Apparently, the Finns appreciated the high magazine capacity and also the strength of the pistol, as it would stand up to use of 9×19mm ammunition intended for the Suomi submachine gun, which was loaded to a higher pressure. It is possible that the High-Power, designated the 9,00 pist/FN in Finnish service, saw action against Soviet forces in the closing stages of the Winter War (November 1939–March 1940) and certainly did during the Continuation War (June 1941–September 1944). Reportedly, some of the High-Powers were issued to Finnish Air Force pilots, often with their

A Finnish High-Power atop the holster supplied along with the stock. The High-Powers continued to be issued until 1985/86, at which point they were declared surplus and sold off (Various 2005). At the time of writing, some FN HP-DA pistols are used by the Finnish Military Police, but Walther P19 and Glock 17 pistols are also used. (Author's Collection)

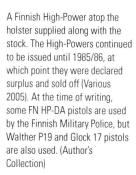

stock/holster. High-Powers were also issued to Finnish Army infantry officers. Quite a few of the holsters originally designed for attachment to stocks were later altered to serve as shoulder holsters when the pistol was carried without the stock.

BELGIAN HIGH-POWERS AT WAR

As was to be expected, though, initial GP 35 production had gone to satisfy Belgian military orders. The first pistols of the initial 10,000 ordered were completed in March 1935. As GP pistols slotted with tangent sights and stocks were delivered for issue to Belgian NCOs and enlisted men, the FN M1900, FN M1910 and Colt M1903 pistols then in use were phased out. It was not until 1939 that commissioned officers started to receive their GP 35 pistols, without shoulder stocks (Vanderlinden 2015b). Although most Belgian NCOs and lower ranks requiring a pistol had received High-Powers by the start of the German invasion of Belgium on 10 May 1940, many Belgian officers had not yet received the upgrade from their previous weapons (Vanderlinden 2013: 304).

A close-up of the markings on a Finnish High-Power: at bottom right, note the 'SA' marking, which stands for *Suomen Armeija* (Finnish Army). As with other weapons used during the Winter and Continuation wars, attrition took its toll on the Finnish High-Powers, with only 1,378 remaining in the country's armouries by 1951. (Courtesy of Rock Island Auction Company)

A right-side view of a pre-World War II FN GP 35, which shows substantial use but still illustrates the wooden grips, tangent sight, ring hammer, non-oval ejection port, half-moon cut and other features of early High-Powers. (Author's Collection)

A pre-World War II Belgian military High-Power holster of typical type that fully encloses the pistol and incorporates a spare-magazine pouch on top of the pistol. (Courtesy of Rock Island Auction Company)

To face the German forces, Belgium could field 550,000 men when fully mobilized. The fighting against German armed forces lasted for 18 days, with the Belgian armed forces suffering 23,350 killed and wounded. When Belgium surrendered to Germany on 28 May 1940, most of the High-Powers that had been issued to its armed forces fell into German hands. Prior to the German occupation of Belgium, a total of 56,500 GP pistols had been manufactured. Captured High-Powers and those produced during the German occupation would see substantial combat with German armed forces during World War II.

One of the fewer than 140 *pistolets de manipulation* (training pistols) produced by FN for the Belgian Army during initial training with the GP 35. The training pistols would have originally been painted red, though examples encountered today rarely have any of the red paint remaining. (Author's Collection)

THE HIGH-POWER IN GERMAN SERVICE

Soon after German armed forces invaded Belgium, the FN factory in Liége was a prime target and as early as 20 May, German officers arrived to take control of it. One important FN official, Dieudonné Saive, escaped to the UK along with a set of drawings for the High-Power (Campbell 2017). Other documents, parts, arms and ammunition were all seized by the German occupiers. Initially, all High-Powers in stock, totalling 3,433 pistols, were inspected and marked with the Waffenamt (Weapons Agency) inspection stamp. Under the supervision of officials from Deutsche Waffen- und Munitionsfabriken (DWM; German Weapons and Munitions Company), production of the GP, now designated the P 640(b), began, with a total of 8,500 produced under German control by the end of 1940. These pistols were marked 'WaA613' (Stevens 1984: 79).

During 1941, 65,700 P 640(b) pistols were produced, including approximately 15,000 assembled from parts on hand. Three different Waffenamt codes were used during 1941: WaA613, WaA103 and WaA140. The last of these codes would remain in use until the Germans abandoned the FN factory in early September 1944 (Stevens 1984: 79).

There is some difficulty in assessing exactly how many P 640(b) pistols were produced during 1942. Although 80,600 were reportedly produced, the actual figure may have been closer to 70,000, the shortfall probably attributed to the lack of enthusiasm of workers for their German masters. Once parts on hand had been exhausted, shortcuts were taken to increase production. The stock slots, tangent sights and magazine safety were eliminated, though not simultaneously. For example, some pistols manufactured under German control had tangent sights but lacked the stock slot (Vanderlinden 2013: 327). It has been suggested that the magazine safety was eliminated partially due to the fact that German military personnel were trained to carry out a magazine change while a round remained in the chamber so that it could be used to engage an enemy in the midst of a reload. In 1943, forced labour was employed, boosting production to 101,000 pistols, though black plastic grips replaced the wooden ones and the quality of finish deteriorated (Stevens 1984: 81).

Despite the use of forced labour, not all of the weapons manufactured for German use at FN were High-Powers. Walther P 38 slides and frames were produced during 1943 and sent to Walther and Metallwarenfabrik Spreewerk in Germany for assembly (Whittington 1976: 103). Ammunition in 6.5×55mm calibre was also produced for Sweden, reportedly to pay for shipments of iron ore received by Germany (Whittington 1976: 104).

Before the German armed forces evacuated Liége in September 1944, an additional 63,000 pistols had been produced. Stevens gives a total figure of 319,000 P 640(b) pistols being produced for the Germans during their control of the FN plant (Stevens 1984: 81). Whittington also gives the figure of 319,000 for the total number of P 640(b) pistols manufactured (Whittington 1976: 102). Ezell states that more than 319,000 pistols were produced for the Germans (Ezell 1981: 224).

The Type I sight on pre-war High-Powers designed for use with a shoulder stock. (Author's Collection)

Adding together the figures given above for production during the German occupation would seem to confirm Ezell's estimate, though it is probably most accurate to say that approximately 319,000 P 640(b) pistols were produced at FN.

Sources generally state that the P 640(b) was issued primarily to *Fallschirmjäger* (airborne) and Waffen-SS personnel (Gander 1998: 161). Issuance to airborne soldiers makes sense, as the higher magazine capacity of the P 640(b) (the box magazines used by the P 08 and P 38 each held only eight rounds) would have made it desirable for troops jumping into combat behind enemy lines, who might lose their primary weapon during a parachute jump. Later in World War II, the *Fallschirmjäger* were issued the FG 42 select-fire automatic rifle, which gave them substantial firepower, but the high-capacity 9×19mm pistol would still have been valued as a secondary weapon. As the Waffen-SS were likely to see more intense combat than many other elements of the German armed forces, once again the reliable, high-capacity P 640(b) would have been a logical issue weapon.

The author can offer one anecdotal story of the P 640(b) in use on the Eastern Front. His first wife was German and during a visit to the USA by her uncle, the author showed him and allowed him to shoot a P 640(b) he owned at the time. The uncle's comment was that he had carried that same type of pistol as a cook on the Eastern Front. The uncle was vague about the unit in which he had served, possibly indicating he had been in a Waffen-SS unit. In any case, the P 640(b) would have been a better defensive weapon for a rear-area soldier on the Eastern Front than one of the small .32-calibre semi-automatics often issued.

THE INGLIS HIGH-POWER

Along with German troops, the armed forces of the British Commonwealth made widespread use of the High-Power during World War II. For the most part, Commonwealth troops that used the High-Power would be issued pistols produced by Inglis of Toronto, Canada. On 3 October 1938, the Inglis Factory in Toronto had signed a contract to build 5,000 Mark I Bren guns for the British War Office. Produced by the Inglis Ordnance Division, the first Bren gun was sent to the UK for trials on 23 March 1940. The first order was followed by subsequent orders, totalling an additional 27,000 Bren guns (Law 2001: 11).

When the FN plant in Liége fell to the Germans on 20 May 1940, the director of FN, Gustave Joassart, and the assistant director, René Laloux, were in London. Importantly, they were eventually joined by Dieudonné Saive, who had been in charge of arms development at FN, and who had completed the design for the High-Power after John Browning's death. When Saive arrived in London in the summer of 1941, he brought with him his design for a semi-automatic military rifle, which later become the FN 49 (Law 2001: 18).

The British asked Saive to create from memory a set of drawings for the High-Power pistol. Upon Saive completing his drawings, the British copied them by 29 June 1943, reportedly with the intent to produce the pistol at Royal Small Arms Factory (RSAF) Enfield (Law 2001: 19). Owing to the exigencies of war, FN's patents were ignored. RSAF Enfield delivered its first prototype based on Saive's drawings on 24 December 1943. Jean Vogel of FN, who had subsequently arrived in the UK, examined the prototype and described it to Saive, noting that he was not sure whether or not the British actually intended to manufacture the High-Power (Law 2001: 22).

FN, of course, was worried that if the British began production of the High-Power, it would make it more difficult to market the GP 35 after the end of the war. In fact, the Belgian engineers declined further assistance to the British without assurances that Belgian rights to the design were affirmed. On 9 February 1944, a letter was sent to Gustave Joassart stating that British production of the High-Power would not take place (Law 2001: 23).

CHINESE HIGH-POWERS

While these events were taking place in the UK, on 27 March 1943, Joassart had written to Val Browning, who was now president of J.M. & M.S. Browning Company of Ogden, Utah, concerning Chiang Kai-shek's regime in China, which had acquired 5,000 High-Powers prior to World War II. China was now interested in obtaining 180,000 High-Power pistols through Canada's Mutual Aid Board, an equivalent of the US Lend Lease Program (Law 2001: 25). Inglis in Toronto would produce the pistols. Joassart stated that in addition to himself, Laloux, Vogel, Saive and Édouard Dufrasne, who had also escaped to the UK, would go to Toronto to supervise the redrafting of production drawings for the High-

Power to be used by Inglis. Because J.M. and M.S. Browning Company owned the rights to Browning designs in North America, Joassart suggested that an agreement on a division of profits could be reached (Stevens 1984: 83–84). Val Browning replied that J.M. and M.S. Browning Company would expect the 5 per cent royalty the firm was due according to pre-war contracts with FN and that his company would want a say in the business of producing semi-automatic pistols in North America after the end of the war. In principle, though, Val Browning supported the importance of the Chinese contract as a means to establish FN in China after the war (Stevens 1984: 85).

Because of his work on the rifle design that would eventually result in the FN 49 and his work on the High-Power drawings while in the UK, the British baulked at Saive going to Canada. While Saive continued to work on the drawings of the High-Power, an agreement was reached whereby Inglis could produce up to 300,000 High-Power pistols (the Chinese order had been increased by another 100,000) with the name 'Browning' on each pistol. Joassart and Laloux travelled to Canada to negotiate details of the deal with Inglis (Stevens 1984: 87).

It should be noted that the need for Saive's presence in Canada was mitigated to some extent by China having supplied six of the FN High-Power pistols they had acquired before the war for Inglis engineers to study. The Inglis engineers also wanted FN drawings to study, however. Additionally, they wanted to consult with the two Belgian engineers they considered to have the most expertise in production of the High-Power: Laloux and Saive (Law 2001: 28).

Canada wanted Laloux and Saive, the UK wanted Saive's drawings; neither was likely to happen quickly unless an agreement was reached for FN to receive royalties. On 4 August 1943, the Canadian government agreed that FN would receive a royalty of 25 cents on each of the 180,000 pistols to be produced for China and 15 cents for each pistol produced in excess of 180,000. After further negotiations, a royalty of 40 cents was agreed for all pistols produced. Another important factor in the agreement was China, the representatives of which wanted the involvement of the FN engineers – an indication of the quality they discerned in their pre-war High-Powers (Law 2001: 30).

CANADA ADOPTS THE HIGH-POWER

It soon became apparent that there would be interest in the Inglis-made High-Power from parties other than China. In September 1943, the Canadian Military Headquarters (CMHQ) in London had cabled Canadian government sources in Ottawa asking for samples of the Inglis High-Power as soon as they were available (Law 2001: 42).

As part of preparations for fulfilling the Chinese contract, beginning in August 1943, Inglis carried out trials using two of the six FN High-Powers supplied by the Chinese from their earlier order. A problem occurred when the early-type round lug cam fractured on one of the pistols, but Laloux explained that there had been a 'fix' for this problem on later-production

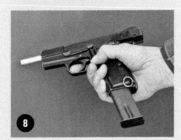

USING THE BROWNING HIGH-POWER

The loaded magazine is inserted into the magazine well (**1**) and pushed home until it locks in place. Note that on this Inglis High-Power the presence of the lanyard ring makes it imperative that the magazine is thrust smartly with the palm of the hand so that the hand doesn't hit the ring, thereby keeping the magazine from seating fully.

The slide is pulled all the way to the rear (**2**) and released to chamber a round. Actually, the best method is to hold the slide firmly and thrust the pistol forward, which makes chambering the round easier as there is less resistance from the spring. The serrations on the slide allow a more secure grip. Note that the finger is off the trigger.

The thumb safety is then applied (**3**). Because the safety on older High-Powers is so small, applying the safety and releasing it is more difficult. The safety cannot be applied unless the hammer is cocked. Some users who have trouble with spring tension when chambering a round, pre-cock the hammer so the slide does not have to push the hammer back to the cocked position when the slide is being pulled to the rear. Prior to firing, the thumb safety must be pushed to the off (down) position (**4**). (The thumb is positioned in this photo to show the safety; in reality, most users push the thumb further forward for more leverage.)

The target is acquired (**5**) using the sights. (As the pistol shown here is an Inglis model, the sights are better and easier to acquire than those of FN pistols of that era.) The pistol is fired (**6**); here, the ejected case can be seen passing in front of the author's sunglasses. Although the recoil is not excessive with a 9×19mm High-Power, the distance the muzzle has risen in firing gives some idea of the time that will be required to fire an aimed repeat shot.

When the magazine is empty the slide locks back (**7**). Visible on the frame to the rear of the trigger, the magazine-release button is pressed (**8**), allowing the magazine to drop free; because of the High-Power's magazine safety it may be necessary to pull it free. Skilled users of the High-Power would often have the spare magazine in their hand so they could strip the empty magazine out of the pistol and by turning the hand over, thrust the reload into place.

Once a loaded magazine has been inserted (**9**), the slide-release lever may be depressed, readying the pistol to fire once again. Note that at this point, the pistol will be loaded and cocked. If immediate engagement is not anticipated the safety can be engaged. If in the middle of a firefight, the pistol will be brought immediately into action.

High-Powers. The committee carrying out the trials also expressed the opinion that the tangent sight and shoulder stock were not of particular value. It was also mentioned in the report that a contract for High-Power pistols to be manufactured for the UK would not require tangent sights or shoulder stocks. In response to reservations about the tangent sight and stock, Laloux commented that those features were incorporated at the request of the purchaser, thus indicating that FN had no problem with pistols being produced without these features (Law 2001: 43–44). It should be noted, however, that the Chinese had considerable experience using the stocked C 96 Mauser and found the stocked High-Power desirable.

Initially, British interest in the Inglis High-Power was to arm Special Operations Executive (SOE) personnel, who preferred 9×19mm pistols for operations in German-occupied areas, so captured ammunition could be used. Nevertheless, SOE had already been in the process of acquiring 8,000 .45 ACP Ballester-Rigaud pistols from Argentina, which they wanted proofed by the Canadians. (Many readers will be more familiar with the designation 'Ballester-Molina', but the pistol was known as the Ballester-Rigaud during 1938–40.) SOE had also been attempting to acquire Luger pistols, though the source or sources of these pistols are not clear (Law 2001: 44).

One of the Chinese High-Powers loaned to Inglis was sent to CMHQ in London for evaluation. The resulting report of 3 December 1943 was favourable. With British and Canadian interest in acquisition of the High-Power, the Belgian production drawings were finally completed and supplied to Inglis in December 1943. On 14 January 1944, the first pre-production Inglis High-Power received its initial firing tests, and on 31 January 1944, the first Chinese production pistol was completed.

With production ready to commence and orders for Inglis High-Powers from both the UK and China, the Canadian Munitions Assignment Committee (CMAC) undertook allocation of production. The first Inglis pistols were scheduled to be completed by February 1944, and the estimate was that 500 pistols would be produced that month, all to go to China. For the remainder of the year China was to be allocated almost two-thirds of production and the UK one-third, with allotment of the estimated 1944 production of pistols to be 142,500: 92,500 for China and 50,000 for the UK. In mid-February, however, the CMAC altered the allotment schedule to raise the proportion of pistols to go to the UK between March and September to complete the UK allotment of 50,000 more rapidly. Total allotment for the entire year remained at 92,500 for China and 50,000 for the UK (Law 2001: 49–51).

To address the British and Canadian desire for a High-Power without the tangent sight, a pistol with just a notch rear sight was built. This pistol was designated the 'No. 2', to differentiate it from the Chinese pistols with tangent sight and shoulder stock designated 'No. 1'. Initially, No. 2 pistols used frames with the slot for a shoulder stock already milled in, but within a short time, No. 2 pistols were produced without the slot (Law 2001: 52). Note that Chinese-contract Inglis No. 1 High-Powers, whether delivered to China or not, can quickly be identified by their serial numbers beginning with 'CH'.

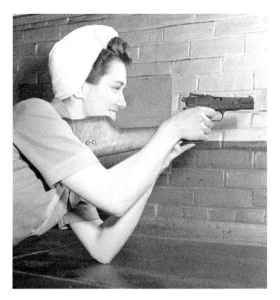 

Although originally anticipated UK sales were to SOE, on 26 July 1944, the British War Office requested 100 Inglis pistols for trials. As the War Office was not interested in the Chinese-contract pistols with tangent sight and shoulder stock, these 100 were pulled from pistols produced for the SOE contract (Law 2001: 64). At least partially as a result of British trials of these pistols – conducted in the UK on 18 August 1944 – and comments from Laloux of FN who had examined them, improvements were made to the pistol, which had been designated the No. 2 Mk I for UK service, after approximately 3,000 had been produced. Changes included: adoption of the square lug barrel cam; an improved ejector; re-shaping of the magazine mouth for better feeding; and taking more care in the removal of external milling marks. The pistols incorporating these improvements were designated Mk 1*. Though they did not bear the 'Mk 1*' designation, pistols intended for China also incorporated these improvements (Stevens 1984: 111).

The Canadian armed forces had also expressed interest in the Inglis High-Power and in May 1944 had received 12 Mk 1* pistols for testing. Combat in Europe after the 6 June 1944 invasion of Normandy proved an impetus for both the British and Canadians to acquire a handgun more effective than the .38-calibre revolvers then in use (Law 2001: 66).

The first 4,000 Inglis High-Powers, marked with Chinese characters, were shipped to China in June 1944, though they met with some disapproval from the Americans, who had equipped Chinese troops with American arms, including .45 ACP M1911 pistols. As a result, the Inglis pistols remained in a warehouse in the port city of Karachi in India awaiting shipment over the Himalayas to China. There was also a belief that the corruption and inefficiency of the Chinese Nationalist regime, as well as the regime's unwillingness to fight the Japanese, warranted a re-evaluation of Canadian aid to China. As a result, a decision was made after 29 July 1944 to suspend deliveries of Inglis High-Powers to China after the first 4,000 had been delivered to Karachi, while another 14,487

ABOVE LEFT
April 1944: A worker at Small Arms Limited in Long Branch, Canada, checks the fit of a shoulder stock for a Chinese-contract Inglis No. 1 pistol. (Library and Archives Canada/ National Film Board of Canada fonds/e000762127)

ABOVE RIGHT
Staff-Sergeant V.H. Dubeau of the 4th Canadian Armoured Brigade Workshop, Royal Canadian Electrical and Mechanical Engineers, inspects a High-Power at Tilburg in the Netherlands, 12 January 1945. (Source: Library and Archives Canada/Department of National Defence fonds/ a168913)

were stored at Longue Pointe Ordnance Depot (LPOD) in Montreal awaiting shipment (Law 2001: 60).

Although it appeared likely that the Chinese contract would be cancelled, the Canadian General Staff requested that the decision of the Mutual Aid Board on cancellation be delayed until the Canadian Army could carry out field trials of the Inglis High-Power for the purpose of adopting it (Law 2001: 67). The Mutual Aid Board agreed not to cancel production without first notifying the Canadian Army. One hundred pistols were sent for Canadian Army trials, with ten retained in Canada and the other 90 sent to the First Canadian Army in Europe. There was some pressure for adoption before Inglis production could be cancelled for lack of a contract. In fact, on 17 September 1944 the Mutual Aid Board informed Canadian military authorities of their intent to cease production of the Inglis High-Power in November or December 1944 (Law 2001: 71).

The 14,487 unshipped Inglis No. 1 pistols of the Chinese contract remained in storage at LPOD until SOE acquired 6,008 of them. The balance of 8,479 pistols remained in storage at LPOD in expectations that the Canadian Army would accept them (Law 2001: 71). According to Law, by January 1945, a total of 13,765 Inglis pistols were supposedly designated for SOE.

Finally, on 3 September 1944, the Canadian Army Overseas (CAO) officially adopted the High-Power manufactured by Inglis. The initial Canadian contract was for 17,500 pistols, many of which were to be supplied from the Chinese pistols that had not been shipped. The remainder would come from the pistols being produced for the British contract, with the Canadian contract being fulfilled by December 1944. In January 1945, however, the Canadian requirement was increased to 25,400 pistols. Although the Canadian order had been for 'fixed sight' No. 2 pistols, to speed acquisition, the CAO accepted the entire stock of Chinese-contract No. 1 pistols remaining at LPOD, receiving 8,479 of

them in January 1945. The remainder of the Canadian contract comprised No. 2 pistols. In March 1945, Canada ordered another 23,300 No. 2 pistols. By May 1945, Canada had received a total of 59,127 Inglis pistols, comprising 8,479 No. 1 pistols left over from the Chinese contract and 50,648 No. 2 pistols (Law 2001: 73–74).

BRITAIN FOLLOWS SUIT

On 26 July 1944, the British War Office had ordered 100 Inglis High-Power pistols for evaluation. Twenty of these pistols, No. 2 Mk 1*s, were used for Ordnance Board trials in October 1944. Though trials of the Inglis High-Power were ongoing, on 26 November 1944, the British War Office issued a requirement for 20,000 Inglis No. 2 Mk 1* pistols for use by the airborne forces (Law 2001: 79). There was sound logic in adoption of the Inglis No. 2 Mk 1* for airborne troops as they were armed with Sten submachine guns, thus easing logistics as 9×19mm ammunition was already in the system.

By the end of 1944, the British requirement was increased to 21,500 pistols for 1945 and another 10,000 for 1946 (Law 2001: 81). Finally, in March 1945 the Ordnance Board issued a positive report on the No. 2 Mk 1* (Law 2001: 88–89).

Shipments of the Inglis High-Power to China were not finished. As part of a second contract, China received 19,000 Inglis pistols between June and September 1945. After the end of the war, another 20,760 Inglis pistols were delivered to LPOD, the final shipment on 19 August 1946. All of the second-contract pistols were of No. 1

Mk 1* type. In total, China had received 43,760 Inglis High-Power pistols (Law 2001: 234). While fighting the Communists for control of China, in 1948, the Nationalists approached Canada about purchasing an additional 18,000 Inglis pistols. However, the Canadians declined to supply any more weapons to China (Law 2001: 235).

According to Stevens, official production of the Inglis High-Power between February 1944 and September 1945, when production ceased, totalled 151,816 pistols (Stevens 1984: 129). According to Law, production was divided between 60,395 No. 1 pistols and 95,661 No. 2 pistols (Law 2001: 265). The agreement between Inglis and FN had stipulated that Canadian production of the High-Power would cease at the end of the war, and this agreement was honoured.

FN AFTER THE GERMAN OCCUPATION

After World War II, FN received orders to rearm Belgian Army troops, beginning in November 1945 (Vanderlinden 2013: 335). FN also began fulfilling foreign contracts again, beginning in 1946 with an unfulfilled pre-World War II contract to produce High-Powers for Denmark. Additional Danish purchases took place in 1958 and 1961 (Vanderlinden 2013: 336). Additional Belgian contracts, including for the Congo, as well as contracts for Austria, Israel, the Netherlands and West Germany, were fulfilled over the next decade.

Until 1950, FN production was devoted to military contracts. Between 1944 and 1950, FN received orders for High-Power pistols from Austria, Belgium, Cambodia, Colombia, Denmark, El Salvador, French Indochina, Indonesia, Lebanon, the Netherlands, Paraguay, Portugal, Syria, the United Kingdom, Venezuela, West Germany and Yugoslavia (Stevens 1984: 153). Many of these countries had used the High-Power prior to World War II or had become familiar with the pistol during the war and were adding to their stockpiles.

One of the High-Powers purchased in 1946 by Denmark after FN resumed production of the pistol. (Author's Collection)

POST-WAR CANADIAN HIGH-POWERS

By the early 1950s, Inglis had turned all of its High-Power tooling over to Canadian Arsenals Limited (CAL) at Long Branch, Ontario. Owned by the Canadian government, CAL was incorporated in 1945 to manage wartime plants and equipment to ensure production facilities would be available to meet the needs of the Department of National Defence (Law 2001: 166). Remaining spare parts were also turned over. Therefore, any modifications or overhauls were carried out at the Arsenal.

One standard overhaul was of No. 1 pistols, which had the tangent-sight assembly removed and the slide machined to accept a new fixed block for a notch rear sight. The block was then brazed to the slide, thus altering any No. 1 pistols to No. 2 configuration. Other early pistols were upgraded to Mk 1* specifications (Stevens 1984: 132). Although it was in contradiction of the agreement with FN, CAL produced at least some No. 2 Mk 1* pistols during the 1950s (Stevens 1984: 134).

Despite the decision not to pursue a lightweight High-Power design (see page 45), CAL had not completely dropped the idea of producing High-Power pistols. In 1955, CAL requested clarification from the Department of Defence Production about negotiating a new agreement with FN to allow production of the pistol in Canada. In 1959 Brigadier-General William J. Lawson, the Judge Advocate General (JAG) of the Canadian Department of National Defence, rendered the opinion that the lack of patents in Canada applying to the Mk 1* indicated that CAL could produce the pistol without negotiating an agreement with FN; however, CAL would have to negotiate with FN to incorporate improvements made in the design since the end of World War II. Lawson also saw no reason why spare parts could not be produced (Law 2001: 187–88).

CAL did begin production of spare parts for Canadian armed forces pistols and for Inglis pistols that had been sold to other countries; but at the point when the cost of a new FN pistol became less than a newly produced CAL barrel, it became no longer economically feasible for CAL to continue with this production (Law 2001: 188).

To keep the Canadian armed forces supplied with Inglis pistols long after the production line had shut down, No. 2 Mk 1* pistols were refurbished. New No. 2 frames were used to replace older No. 1 frames slotted for the shoulder stock. Reportedly, these modifications were performed on fewer than 200 pistols (Law 2001: 189).

An Inglis No. 1 with shoulder stock attached and an Inglis No. 2 Mk 1* with canvas holster. During World War II, SOE supplied pistols to partisans fighting against the Germans. By the end of November 1944, Greek resistance fighters had received at least 2,820 Inglis pistols; all of these were No. 2 type, 2,500 of them the No 2 Mk 1* type. When Greek resistance groups were incorporated into the new Hellenic Army after the end of World War II, many of the Inglis pistols would have gone with them. To supply later High-Power pistols to Greek troops, FN High-Powers were acquired. (Author's Collection)

On 30 June 1976, the Small Arms Division of CAL was closed and Diemaco, Inc. of Kitchener, Ontario took over responsibility for the upkeep and development of Canadian small arms. This affected the High-Powers in service with the Canadian armed forces, as Diemaco received a contract during the 1980s to inspect, repair and overhaul all of the Inglis High-Powers in Canadian military inventories (Law 2001: 191). Diemaco also experimented with modernizing the Inglis pistols in use by upgrading existing High-Powers using available parts such as ambidextrous safeties and rubber wraparound grips to produce a 'Production Improved Product' High-Power. There are no indications that these improvements were ever carried out on a large scale, however (Law 2001: 193).

LIGHTENING THE HIGH-POWER

While overhauling the Inglis No. 1 pistols for the Canadian armed forces, Canadian Arsenals Limited (CAL) was also experimenting with producing a lightweight version of the Mk 1*. Reportedly, development of the lightweight pistol had begun as a result of US Army interest during 1947 in an Inglis High-Power but of lighter weight. By March 1948, CAL had received six alloy frames on which were built prototype pistols for evaluation by US, Canadian and British armed forces. Slides for the pistols were standard production examples with lightening cuts (Law 2001: 170–71). Two of these prototype pistols were sent to the UK for testing at the Proof and Experimental Establishment at Pendine, Wales. In the USA, Springfield Armory carried out trials of the two lightweight pistols supplied, while in Canada, the Directorate of Armament Development carried out trials of the two lightweight pistols supplied to it. None of the entities that tested the lightweight High-Power expressed serious interest in it, however (Law 2001: 169–80).

Jean Vogel of FN learned of these experimental lightweight pistols, which in February 1952 caused FN to register a complaint that the Canadians were in violation of the terms of the agreement allowing them to produce High-Power pistols (Stevens 1984: 134).

A lightweight model was also produced with a shortened slide in an attempt to reduce weight further and make the pistol easier to carry (Stevens 1984: 142–44). Neither of the lightweight projects went past the prototype stage. It is worth noting, though, that FN did later produce a lightweight version of the High-Power.

Post-war requirements for a new service pistol established by both the USA and the UK specified a pistol weighing less than 25oz (709g)

Weighing 714g, the subsequent Lightweight High-Power was built with an alloy frame, but otherwise resembled the standard High-Power pistol. (Author's Collection)

and having a double action (Law 2001: 180). Presumably, experience with the German P 38 in World War II had influenced the desire for a double-action pistol. During 1949, CAL examined the feasibility of incorporating a double-action mechanism into the Mk 1*, but concluded that it would require a complete redesign of the pistol (Law 2001: 181).

Despite their expressed interest in a lighter pistol with a double-action mechanism, the US and UK armed forces continued to use the Colt M1911 and the High-Power respectively for decades. Canada had concluded in the years when CAL was evaluating the lightweight frame for the Mk 1* and the feasibility of a double-action model that with approximately 37,000 High-Power pistols on hand, the expense of adopting a lightweight double-action design was prohibitive (Law 2001: 181).

Prototype of a post-World War II lightweight Inglis High-Power.
(Courtesy of Rock Island Auction Company)

INGLIS PISTOLS IN OTHER HANDS

One of the more interesting recipients of the Inglis High-Power pistol after World War II was Belgium. In 1950, Canada transferred war-surplus equipment to other NATO powers. This included complete equipment for one infantry division (Canada's Defence Appropriations Act of 1950 allowed the gift or sale of equipment to arm an infantry division to fellow NATO countries), including 1,578 High-Power pistols. Canada used this transfer to get rid of at least some of the Inglis No. 1 High-Powers still in the armouries. (As Belgian documentation described the pistols as having tangent sights, it may be presumed that all or a substantial portion of the pistols were of the No. 1 type.) As FN post-war production of High-Powers became sufficient for Belgian needs, the Inglis pistols became reserve stock or were issued to the Gendarmerie Royale. Many of the Inglis pistols held by Belgium were later sold on the surplus market during the 1980s (Law 2001: 227).

Belgium's neighbour the Netherlands also received Inglis High-Power pistols after World War II. As Canada cut back its armed forces dramatically at the end of the conflict, a large volume of surplus arms and equipment became available. As a result, in 1946, 10,000 Inglis pistols were sold to the Netherlands, which designated them Pistool 46. The shipment was comprised primarily of No. 2 Mk 1* models, but there also seem to have been some No. 1 Mk 1* pistols mixed in (Law 2001: 241–42). In 1950, Canada gifted the Netherlands an additional 1,578 Inglis pistols (Law 2001: 242). In 1951, the Netherlands requested another 20,000 Inglis High-Powers, but Inglis was no longer producing pistols and Canadian stocks of surplus pistols had been depleted. As a result, the Dutch ordered the additional pistols they needed from FN (Law 2001: 245).

By the mid-1950s, the presence of two types of High-Power pistol – Inglis and FN – became problematical, as an issue arose with parts interchangeability, especially of barrels. New FN barrels would not fit the Inglis pistols (Law 2001: 246). Although it was possible to alter the Inglis pistols to accept an FN barrel, to do so would require each Dutch Inglis pistol to be sent for alteration. Dutch armourers had maintained inventories of both Inglis and FN parts, but stocks of the Inglis parts were running low and the cost of obtaining them from CAL was prohibitive. FN came to the rescue by offering to modify the Inglis High-Powers to FN specifications, thus allowing parts interchangeability, for the cost of 525 Belgian Francs each (Law 2001: 246). The Dutch High-Powers, of both types, continued in use until adoption of the Glock pistol in 1993 (Law 2001: 253).

Other countries purchased Inglis High-Powers from Canadian inventories after World War II. In May 1962, 500 Inglis No. 2 pistols were shipped to New Zealand. When New Zealand wanted to purchase an additional 372 Inglis pistols in 1965, however, the Canadians were unwilling to deplete their stocks of the pistols any further, which resulted in New Zealand ordering L9A1 pistols from FN instead (Law 2001: 258). In the 1980s, the Inglis pistols were withdrawn from New Zealand service, followed in 1992 by replacement of the remaining L9A1 High-Powers with the SIG Sauer P226 (Law 2001: 260). New Zealand has since adopted the Glock 17, but some SIG Sauer P226 pistols remain in service. While Inglis and FN L9A1 pistols remain in Australian service today, its special-forces personnel use the HK USP.

An Inglis No. 2 Mk 1* High-Power along with a Belgian-style holster; Inglis High-Powers were used by Belgium after World War II while FN was getting the FN High-Power back into production. (Author's Collection)

THE HIGH-POWER IN EUROPE

Having adopted the Inglis High-Power during World War II, the British acquired additional Inglis High-Powers in the decade after 1945. In the 1950s, however, the UK also ordered FN High-Powers. These pistols are identifiable by their serial number beginning with the letter 'E'. In 1964, an order was placed for FN High-Powers incorporating an external extractor. This version was adopted as the L9A1 and the order specified that these pistols have the NSN (NATO stock number) on major parts such as the frame, slide, barrel and magazine. Additionally, the year of manufacture and 'FN' were marked on the slide, barrel and magazine. The slide markings incorporated 'PISTOL AUTOMATIC L9A1'. Later orders did not always incorporate the NSN or the 'L9A1' marking (Vanderlinden 2013: 347).

Beyond the UK and Belgium (where the FN-produced GP 35 or L9A1 has been succeeded by the FN Five-seveN), the High-Power has also been used by the armed forces and/or law-enforcement agencies of Austria (FN GP 35 used by the Gendarmerie; the current standard military firearm is the Glock 17), Cyprus, Denmark (GP 35 purchased from FN and designated the P M/46; the current standard pistol is the SIG Sauer P320), Estonia (FN GP 35; currently uses the HK USP), Finland, France (the FN GP 35 was used by the Gendarmerie Nationale and French Air Force in Indochina and Algeria; the primary handgun of French armed forces was the MAC Mle 50 for many years, but this was replaced by the PAMAS G1 (the French version of the Beretta 92); French special forces use the HK USP), Greece (Inglis pistols; the principal weapon currently is the HK USP, made under licence by EAS), Hungary (FÉG MOD PJK-9HP; current standard weapon is the P9RC, a domestically produced pistol similar in appearance to the GP 35), Ireland (FN GP 35; current issue weapon is the HK USP), Lithuania (FN GP 35; current issue pistol is the Glock 17),

British military-issue L9A1 pistol with its NATO catalogue number on the slide. Serving alongside the L9A1, the SIG Sauer P226 (L105A1) and P228 (L107A1) were purchased for use in Afghanistan during the UK's participation in Coalition operations in that country after 2001. In addition to serving as the standard UK service pistol until the adoption of the Glock 17 Gen 4 as the L131A1 in 2013, the L9A1 was also adopted by Commonwealth countries including Australia, Botswana, India, Malaya/Malaysia, Nepal and New Zealand. Though many parts were not interchangeable, Canada continued to use Inglis High-Powers as well as FN High-Powers for many years. (Author's Collection)

ABOVE LEFT
A Belgian police officer carrying an FN High-Power is aided by medical personnel after violence at the European Cup Final on 29 May 1985, pitting Juventus against Liverpool. During the confrontation between rival fans, 39 people – mostly Italians – lost their lives, with a further 600 being injured. The author spent time with friends from the Belgian Police shortly after this incident, and feelings ran very strong that much tougher measures were needed to counter British football hooliganism. (Liverpool Echo/ Mirrorpix/Getty Images)

ABOVE RIGHT
March 1973: an off-duty British NCO remains alert with his L9A1 pistol in West Belfast, Northern Ireland. (Alex Bowie/Getty Images)

Luxembourg, the Netherlands, Poland (GROM, Poland's special-forces unit, formerly used the FN P 35, likely because of SAS influence; the 9×18mm P-83 Wanad and WIST-94 pistols were used, with the Polish PR-15 Ragun about to replace the WIST-94 at the time of writing), Portugal (FN GP 35; current service pistols include the Walther P 38, SIG Sauer P228 and HK USP) and Romania (the GP 35 was used before World War II; at the time of writing, the domestically produced M1995 and its upgrade, the M2000, are used). In the case of Lithuania, Luxembourg, the Netherlands and the UK, the Glock 17 has been chosen to replace the High-Power.

BRITISH SPECIAL FORCES AND THE HIGH-POWER

The UK's Special Air Service (SAS) used the High-Power for decades when operating undercover, as on 'Keeni-Meeni' operations targeting assassins in Aden during 1963–67. When the SAS's Counter Revolutionary Warfare Wing was formed in the early 1970s for counter-terrorist operations, the High-Power was selected as a back-up to the HK MP5 submachine gun. Among the innovations made by the SAS when using the High-Power for counter-terrorist operations was adoption of the 20-round extended magazine and use of a wrist carrier for a spare magazine for quicker access. SAS troops, as well as British intelligence personnel, were often armed with the High-Power during missions in Northern Ireland. One notable use of the High-Power by the SAS was during Operation *Flavius*, when SAS operators killed three members of the Provisional Irish Republican Army (PIRA) on Gibraltar on 6 March 1988.

For the SAS and Special Boat Service, as well as the Special Reconnaissance Regiment, the pistol is a more important weapon than for conventional infantry. Prior to the adoption of the SIG Sauer P226 or P228 for British special-forces personnel, the High-Power was used for various purposes. For special operators deployed in areas where they might be carrying out surveillance wearing local clothing, the High-Power could be readily concealed. Operators on missions behind enemy lines or in contested areas relied upon the High-Power should their rifle malfunction or run out of ammunition in combat. Operators were trained to transition immediately to their pistol to keep fighting. There have been cases reported during the 'War on Terror' in which an operator has sustained a wound to a hand or arm that has made it necessary to transition to the handgun because it becomes difficult to fire the rifle. When operating from civilian vehicles, the pistol could also be brought into action more readily from within the vehicle than many rifles or carbines. Special-forces snipers also carried the pistol for use at closer quarters when it was not expedient or practical to deploy their long-range marksman's weapon.

Another instance in which the High-Power (or more recently the SIG Sauer or Glock) has been used by special forces is during hostage-rescue or building-clearance operations. An operator covering those team members breaching a door with a ballistic shield may deploy the pistol more readily with one hand.

Members of Britain's 14th Intelligence Company, both male and female, each carried at least one High-Power and often two on undercover missions in Northern Ireland from 1973 on. Reportedly, 14th Intelligence Company personnel had extended safeties added to their High-Powers to allow them to engage more quickly. One source states that these extended safeties were from the Cylinder and Slide Shop. It is not clear if 14th Intelligence Company had the magazine safeties removed from their High-Powers to speed reloads, but New Zealand SAS armourers reportedly removed these safeties and marked the pistols 'M' for modified (Various 2009). In some cases, 14th Intelligence Company operators had a High-Power with a 20-round magazine secreted in their vehicle in case they encountered a PIRA roadblock and needed to access a weapon quickly.

FAR LEFT
Pictured in July 1982, this British Army corporal is firing an L9A1 High-Power. Female soldiers assigned to 14th Intelligence Company in Northern Ireland sometimes carried two High-Powers, one with an extended magazine located in their vehicle. (Barry James Gilmour/Fairfax Media via Getty Images)

LEFT
The L9A1 High-Power was a constant companion to many British Army soldiers serving in Northern Ireland. Pictured in West Belfast during May 1973, this Army Intelligence officer holsters his L9A1 before leaving base. (Alex Bowie/Getty Images)

A member of the Special Air Service Special Projects Team armed with an MP5 submachine gun and a High-Power pistol. He wears his spare magazine in a special wrist carrier to allow fast access. (Author's Collection)

Because they were operating undercover in a dangerous environment, operators of 14th Intelligence Company had to be especially skilled with their weapons. As a result, they received even more intensive training with their High-Powers than did the SAS. As their personal weapon, they were issued a High-Power with a covert waistband holster and a magazine pouch containing two spare magazines. They were trained to have their pistol close at hand at all times when operating in Northern Ireland. Unlike other British military units that carried their pistols with an empty chamber, 14th Intelligence Company operators carried theirs with a round chambered and 'cocked and locked' (the hammer cocked and the safety on). Operators were allowed to carry the pistol in whatever position gave them quickest access, including in a shoulder holster. During their training, they were told that the High-Power was chosen for its reliability, stopping power and 9×19mm chambering – the same chambering as their HK MP5 submachine guns (Rennie 1996: 90–91).

Operators were trained to fire accurate 'double taps' to head or chest at 25yd (23m). They were also trained to count rounds so that they could ensure that a round remained in the chamber, ready to fire if necessary during a reload. (For this technique to be viable, the magazine safety would have to be disabled on the pistol.) As is standard in combat pistol training, operators were taught to carry out instant malfunction drills, though Rennie notes that the High-Powers were so reliable that instructors had to cause artificial malfunctions by inserting inert drill rounds into magazines (Rennie 1996: 93).

So well-trained were 14th Intelligence Company operators that one member of the unit when stopped by PIRA members armed with Armalite (M16) rifles used his 'car High-Power', which was loaded with a 20-round magazine, to put four rounds into the PIRA man pointing a rifle at him through the driver's window. He then rolled out of the door and killed a second terrorist at the rear of the car with multiple rounds. As the 14th Intelligence Company operator re-entered his vehicle, he came under fire from a third PIRA man exiting his vehicle and wounded that man before speeding away. The quick reactions and skill with his High-Power saved the operator's life and proved the value of his training. Although the operator did not use the technique in this encounter, 14th Intelligence Company operators were trained to shoot PIRA members operating illegal checkpoints through the car door to keep the element of surprise while engaging (Rennie 1996: 162–63).

Other British soldiers in Northern Ireland carried the High-Power when in civilian clothing. For example, when British Army corporals Derek Wood and David Howes drove into a PIRA funeral procession on 19 March 1988, the crowd of mourners attacked them. Although the two soldiers were armed with L9A1 pistols and Wood fired a shot in the air, they did not fire at the crowd and were subsequently killed. Had the two soldiers chosen to resist the attack, their pistols with 13-round magazine capacities would have ensured a substantial number of PIRA sympathizers died with them. On 2 August 1988, one of the High-Power pistols taken from the slain soldiers was used to kill Lance-Corporal Roy Butler of the Ulster Defence Regiment in Belfast.

ROYAL MILITARY POLICE CLOSE PROTECTION TEAMS

Royal Military Police (RMP) Close Protection personnel protect high-ranking officers as well as UK diplomats around the world. RMP Close Protection personnel also supplement protection officers from Royalty and Specialist Protection Branch in some instances when members of the Royal Family visit high-threat environments.

From the time the Browning High-Power replaced Webley or S&W .38 revolvers with the RMP until 2001, when the SIG Sauer P226 replaced it, the High-Power was the standard handgun used by RMP Close Protection teams. According to Keightley, the High-Power was issued with two magazines and no magazine pouch, so the spare magazine was

Conversion units in .22 calibre allowed inexpensive training with the High-Power. This one from Pachmayr is considered one of the best. (Author's Collection)

carried in a pocket; shoulder holsters were normally used when team members were operating in plain clothes (Keightley 2014: 84). The Sterling submachine gun was also carried when concealment was not necessary or as a support weapon in a vehicle. In some cases, the RMP bodyguards had to make do with just their High-Powers. In 1970, for example, a pair of RMP Close Protection NCOs armed with just their High-Powers were assigned to protect Prime Minister Edward Heath who was visiting West Germany (Keightley 2014: 84).

Although the High-Power was issued to RMP Close Protection personnel because it was a standard British Army weapon, it also was a sound handgun choice for close protection because its high-capacity magazine allowed the bodyguard to engage attackers more effectively while providing covering fire during an evacuation of the principal (the person being protected). Many of those who worked in close-protection teams during the 1960s–1980s, including the author, chose the High-Power for this reason and often carried spare 20-round magazines to enable longer sustained suppressive fire with the pistol.

ARMED METROPOLITAN POLICE UNITS AND THE HIGH-POWER

Tony Long was an armed member of the London Metropolitan Police from 1973, when the S&W .38 Special Model 10 revolver was the standard handgun, but by 1990 the Glock 17 had been adopted. In his book *Lethal Force*, Long discusses the deployment of armed officers and their use of weapons. He served with D11, which served both to train police officers in the use of firearms and to act as a response unit to contain armed criminals. D11 became known as PT17 in 1987. The principal handgun in use with D11 and later PT17 was the Browning High-Power. Members of PT17 also used the HK MP5 submachine gun. Long notes that members of PT17 shot their High-Powers well enough that members of the SAS were impressed when the units undertook joint training (Long 2016: 96). Interestingly, in 1988, it was agreed that royalty protection officers would be issued the High-Power to give them more firepower when protecting members of the British Royal Family. It is unclear, however, whether the pistols were ever issued as the Royalty Protection Unit was using Glock 17 pistols by 1991 (Waldren 2007: 150–51).

Tony Long carried his High-Power concealed on assignments such as staking out a security van reported to be the target of armed robbers in support of the Flying Squad (Long 2016: 120). On Christmas Day 1985, Long saved a young girl's life when he shot a hostage-taker who had just plunged a knife into her shoulder. For this operation, Long had chosen to use a S&W Model 19 revolver rather than his High-Power because of the greater stopping power of the Model 19's hollow-point .357 Magnum ammunition. He stopped the hostage-taker with a double tap to the exposed part of his body followed by a single shot to the head. Although it is likely that the same three-shot combination from the High-Power would have stopped the hostage-taker from continuing to stab the child,

The Glock 17 Gen 4. After using the High-Power throughout his service with D11 and PT17, Tony Long was tasked with evaluating the Glock 17 as a possible replacement for the High-Power. After using it for a month, he recommended that it be adopted (Long 2016: 196–97). In 1990 the Glock 17 became the standard sidearm for armed officers of the Metropolitan Police, though some plainclothes officers have been issued the more compact Glock 26. (Author's Collection)

the fully jacketed 9×19mm rounds may have had less effect. Though the .357 Magnum round stopped his hostile acts, the hostage-taker survived to stand trial (Long 2016: 137–47).

Long went back to his High-Power carried concealed for other stakeouts of expected security-van robberies, possibly because if a firefight ensued, the higher capacity of the High-Power would be appreciated, but more likely because it was the standard-issue weapon. On 15 July 1987, 19 months after he had shot the hostage-taker, Long downed two armed robbers targeting a security van with double taps from his High-Power (Long 2016: 162–63).

THE HIGH-POWER IN THE AMERICAS

While Inglis-produced versions of the High-Power remain in Canadian service, also on issue are the SIG Sauer P225/226 and HK USP (for special-operations forces). As of 2017, reportedly, there were still 13,981 Inglis High-Power pistols serving with the Canadian armed forces; 1,243 of those were scheduled for cannibalization to obtain spare parts, however. There is intent to replace the Inglis with a new General Service Pistol, but it appears that a new pistol will not be approved and deliveries begin until 2022 or later (Pugliese 2017).

Beyond Canada, the High-Power has been widely used by countries right across the Americas. Countries using the High-Power include Argentina, Barbados (FN GP 35), Belize (L9A1), Bermuda (FN GP 35 or L9A1), Bolivia (FN- and FMAP-produced High-Powers as well as the Beretta 92F and Glock 17), Brazil (High-Power reportedly used but not confirmed; current issue weapons are the Taurus PT-92, Imbel GC and Glock 17), Chile (FN GP 35; the current primary-issue handgun is the FAMAE FN-750, a locally produced version of the CZ 75), Colombia (FN GP 35; the current issue weapon is the domestically produced Cordova), Cuba (FN GP 35; current standard weapon is the 9×18mm Makarov PM), Dominican Republic (the FN GP 35 still appears to be in

The crest on the slide of an Argentine Navy High-Power. In the Falklands War in 1982, Argentinian troops armed with the FM faced British troops armed with the L9A1. Reportedly, captured British High-Powers were used by the Argentinians; more often, British troops not normally authorized a pistol would use captured Argentinian High-Powers, some of which were brought back as war trophies. The High-Power remains in Argentine service today alongside the Bersa Thunder and Glock variants. (Author's Collection)

RIGHT
A Uruguayan Marine armed with the High-Power, most likely produced by FMAP. During a training exercise in April 2009, the Marine is preparing to carry out a practice room-clearing entry through the door at the left of photograph. Uruguay's armed forces use the FMAP-produced High-Power alongside the Glock 17 and HK P30. (Lance Cpl Abby Burtner/Wikimedia/Public Domain)

FAR RIGHT
Full-auto bursts fired at a hostage-taker target at 7yd (6.4m) with the select-fire High-Power; a 20-round magazine of the type used by the FBI and others is in place. (Author's Collection)

use, but more recently the Browning BDM and Taurus PT-92 have also been acquired), Ecuador (FN GP 35 alongside the Beretta 92F and SIG Sauer P226), El Salvador (initially, FN GP 35, but more recently the Argentine FM; appears to still be in use but various other modern military handguns from Glock, Beretta and SIG Sauer have also been acquired), Guatemala, Haiti, Honduras (FN GP 35 as well as the SIG Sauer P226, Beretta 92FS and CZ 75), Panama, Paraguay (the HK P9 has also been used), Peru (the GP 35 still appears to be in service along with the Beretta 92), Surinam, Trinidad and Tobago, Uruguay and Venezuela.

THE FBI HOSTAGE RESCUE TEAM AND THE BROWNING HIGH-POWER

In the USA, the FN GP 35 has been used by intelligence agencies and special-operations forces. Probably influenced to at least some extent by the fact that the SAS employed the High-Power, when the FBI Hostage Rescue Team (HRT) was formed in 1983 it also used the High-Power pistol. Between 1986 and 1990, c.250 pistols were built by custom pistolsmith Wayne Novak. Alterations included installation of the Novak Lo-Mount three-dot night sight and Spegel grips. Other work, done on some of the pistols, included the addition of front straps with a matte finish, beavertail frame modifications, match barrels and a trigger job. In some cases, trigger work was done by FBI gunsmiths at Quantico, Virginia. As with the SAS, the FBI also used 20-round magazines unless the High-Powers were being carried concealed.

In his book *No Errors*, Danny Coulson, founder of the FBI HRT, offers an interesting insight as to how one adversary of the HRT viewed the High-Power pistol carried by the agents. During an attempt to end a stand-off with The Covenant, the Sword, and the Arm of the Lord (CSA), a paramilitary anti-government group, Coulson had a meeting with James Ellison, the CSA leader, in an attempt to end the siege peacefully. Ellison recognized the High-Powers being carried by HRT members and queried why they chose it over the .45 semi-automatic. In an attempt to keep Ellison talking the agents explained that they chose the 9×19mm High-Power, even though it fired a smaller bullet, because they were trained to place their shots exactly where they wanted them. They also explained they liked the fact that they could carry the High-Power with a round chambered and 'cocked and locked' (the hammer cocked and the safety on) as it was faster. Ellison was impressed as carrying the weapon 'cocked and locked' indicated that the agents were real professionals. This perception of the HRT may have helped convince Ellison and his followers to surrender peacefully (Coulson 1999: 296).

THE HIGH-POWER IN AFRICA

The High-Power has seen widespread service during the many wars in Africa since 1945. Notably, the Force Publique, a militarized gendarmerie composed of Belgian officers and indigenous troops in the Congo, used the High-Power. Personnel of the Ministry of Finance, including customs and other officials, also used High-Powers in the Congo during the colonial era. Pistols intended for the Force Publique were marked 'F.P' and had the Belgian Congo crest, while those used by the Ministry of Finance were marked 'ETAT' or 'C.B.' for Congo Belge. After the Congo achieved independence on 30 June 1960, additional High-Powers were purchased from FN for the new country. These were marked 'ANC' for Armée nationale congolaise (Vanderlinden 2013: 341). At least some of these High-Powers were subsequently captured or stolen and used by mercenary troops or insurgents such as the 'Simbas' during the fighting in the Congo between 1960 and 1965. In what is now the Democratic Republic of the Congo (formerly Zaire), the current standard-issue pistol is the Russian Tokarev TT.

High-Powers have also been carried in Angola by the forces of the Frente Nacional de Libertacão de Angola (more recently the Tokarev TT-33 and Makarov PM have been issued), Botswana (FN-produced High-Powers, possibly acquired from the UK), Burundi, Cameroon, Chad (as well as the wz. 35 Vis Radom, MAC Mle 50 and Tokagypt 58, among others), Ghana, Kenya, Liberia (via Fargo International), Malawi (L9A1, of UK origin), Mozambique (FN GP 35, alongside the Makarov PM, 9×18mm Stechkin, Tokarev and Walther P 38), Namibia (as well as the Makarov PM and CZ 75), Nigeria (locally produced under licence by Defence Industries Corporation of Nigeria; also in use are the Beretta M92 and M1951 and the Walther P5), Rwanda, Sierra Leone, South Africa (FN GP 35; current issue pistols include the Vektor Z-88, a domestically produced version of the Beretta M92, and the Vektor SP1), Sudan, Tanzania (alongside the Stechkin), Togo (as well as the .357 Manurhin MR 73 and MAB PA15), Tunisia, Uganda (as well as the Tokarev TT) and Zimbabwe (alongside the Tokarev TT).

Among the Belgian colonial contracts received by FN after World War II were those for High-Power pistols to arm the Force Publique in the Congo. Some records are missing, but total Force Publique orders may have totalled 1,700. This is a view of the top of a Force Publique High-Power showing the Belgian crest. (Author's Collection)

THE MOZAMBIQUE DRILL

One African encounter featuring a High-Power during the Mozambican War of Independence (1964–74) led to a new firing drill. At Lourenço Marques (now Maputo International) Airport, Rhodesian mercenary Mike Rousseau faced a Frente de Libertação de Moçambique fighter armed with an AK-47 assault rifle. Rousseau only had his High-Power, so he shot the guerrilla twice in the chest but failed to stop him, probably because he was using 115-grain (7.45g) full-metal-jacketed loads in his High-Power. He finally fired at the guerrilla's head, hitting him the neck, thus severing his spinal column and ending the fight.

As a result of hearing of this encounter, well-known US firearms trainer Jeff Cooper developed a drill that entailed firing two rounds to the chest and a third to the head. If the first two rounds failed to end the fight, the third to the head would. Because of where the fight occurred that inspired the drill, it came to be known as the 'Mozambique Drill'. It is still used by many special-operations units today in case an enemy is wearing body armour (Dabbs 2018).

March 2011: a Libyan man points a High-Power in the air in Tobruk, Libya, during the Libyan Civil War. The pistol is probably of FN origin and appears to be nickel plated, but is possibly gold plated as were some pistols owned by high-ranking Libyan officials. Former Libyan leader Muammar Gaddafi was carrying a gold-plated High-Power when he was captured and killed on 20 October 2011. Libyan forces were issued the FN GP 35 and currently carry the Italian Beretta 92FS and the Serbian CZ 99. (Joe Raedle/Getty Images)

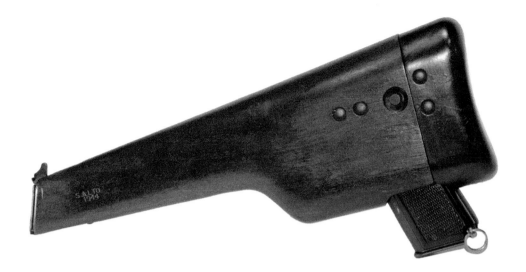

THE HIGH-POWER IN ASIA

As has been mentioned already, Nationalist Chinese forces made widespread use of High-Powers during the latter stages of the Second Sino-Japanese War (1937–45) and the Chinese Civil War (1927–50). During the Korean War (1950–53), it is entirely likely that some Communist Chinese troops used High-Powers that had been captured from the Nationalists, while Commonwealth troops fighting on the UN side were armed with the High-Power. The Communist Chinese captured substantial numbers of Inglis High-Powers, many of which remained in service until at least the 1980s. Some were supplied by China to 'liberation movements' such as the Viet Cong in Vietnam. Those High-Powers remaining in China were eventually sold as surplus, often after having been arsenal refurbished and refinished.

Elsewhere in Asia, the High-Power has equipped troops from Bangladesh (the L9A1 is still in use alongside the 7.62×25mm Chinese Type 54), Brunei, Cambodia (the GP 35; current-issue weapons include the Type 54, Tokarev TT-33 and Makarov PM), China (unlicensed

An Inglis High-Power in the Small Arms Limited stock designed for the Chinese contract. (Author's Collection)

The High-Power in the Chinese Civil War (overleaf)

On 25–27 October 1949, 9,000 members of the PLA (People's Liberation Army) attempted to land on Kinman Island, which was under control of the Republic of China. As the PLA forces moved inland, they came under fire from M5A1 tanks of the ROC 18th Army. Heavy fighting took place at Shaungru Hill, held by the PLA 244th Regiment. As the ROC tanks advanced the survivors of the 244th Regiment were driven back towards the beaches, but the PLA troops could not be evacuated because the transports had been grounded by the tide going out. During their defeat the PLA forces suffered 3,873 killed and 5,175 captured, while the ROC troops suffered 1,267 killed and 1,982 wounded. This illustration shows a portion of the battle near the beaches as the PLA is driven back by ROC troops. The ROC troops are primarily armed with US-supplied M1903A3 rifles and Thompson submachine guns; the ROC officer in the foreground, however, is armed with an Inglis High-Power with the holster stock attached.

THE HIGH-POWER IN VIETNAM

Special-operations troops of the US Military Assistance Command Vietnam/Special Operations Group (MACV/SOG) were issued FN High-Power pistols as 'sterile' (untraceable) weapons when they carried out cross-border and other clandestine operations during the Vietnam War. MACV/SOG High-Powers were obtained through the Central Intelligence Agency.

According to MACV/SOG expert John Plaster, a few of the MACV/SOG High-Powers were chrome plated and boxed as a 'Reconnaissance Team Leader Recognition Award'. Some of the recipients were also winners of the Congressional Medal of Honor (Plaster 2016).

US 'tunnel rats', who entered and cleared Viet Cong tunnel complexes, sometimes used the High-Power as its larger magazine capacity allowed a lot of shots to be fired quickly in the close quarters of the tunnels. Some of the High-Powers used by troops in Vietnam such as tunnel rats or helicopter pilots were reportedly purchased at a post exchange (shop at a US military camp) on Okinawa.

Various sources, including US GIs who brought back captured High-Powers, reported that the Viet Cong were also armed with High-Powers, likely including those supplied by Communist China, possibly ones captured by the Soviets from German armed forces, or acquired from other sources. As some sources state that the High-Powers encountered during the Vietnam War had Chinese markings, they may have been referring to those from the Inglis Nationalist Chinese contract that had been captured by the Communist Chinese.

Norinco copies), India (the domestically produced 1A; some FN GP 35 pistols may also be in service; currently, special-forces units have the SIG Sauer P226 and Glock 17), Indonesia (the Pindad P1A, an unlicensed copy of the GP 35; currently, the Pindad P2 is also issued, as are at least some HS2000 pistols), Malaysia (the L9A1, with special forces issued the Beretta 92 and Glock 17), Myanmar (the GP 35 remains in use alongside some Glock 17 and SIG Sauer P226 pistols), Nepal, North Korea (High-Power use by special forces is reported; various pistols are widely issued, including the locally made Type 66 copy of the Makarov PM and Type 68 copy of the Tokarev TT-30), Pakistan (reported use by Naval Special Service Group, but origin unknown; SSG also uses the SIG Sauer P226, Glock 17 and HK P7; the locally produced POF PK-09 is a Beretta 92 copy and appears to be standard issue), the Philippines (GP 35; as of 2017, the Glock 17 was adopted for general issue), Singapore (GP 35; principal issue handgun is the SIG Sauer P226), Sri Lanka (GP 35; more recent weapons include the Beretta 92, Glock 17 and Glock 19), Taiwan (GP 35; principal current-issue pistol is the locally produced T75K1,

Afghanistan 2012 (opposite)

On 14 September 2012, 15 Taliban fighters disguised as Afghan soldiers carried out a raid on Camp Bastion, the major British base in Afghanistan. After penetrating the base, Taliban fighters engaged US Marine Corps mechanics from VMM-161 and also attacked aircraft refuelling stations. USMC aircraft were attacked using explosive charges and rocket-propelled grenades. After a four-hour firefight, all Taliban were either killed or captured by US Marines or members of 51 Squadron, RAF Regiment. Fire support was supplied by British Apache AH1 and USMC AH-1W SuperCobra helicopters. This plate depicts members of the RAF Regiment responding to the attack. All members of the RAF Regiment were equipped with the L85A2 rifle; however, the dog handler has his slung on his back and due to the need to control his dog has drawn his L9A1 High-Power to engage the enemy.

SELECT-FIRE HIGH-POWERS

Although the High-Power was not intended to function as a machine pistol, some have been altered to fire on full-auto. They have seen use in the Middle East and also in Latin America, where some drug lords have shown an affinity for carrying them.

Registered full-auto High-Powers have also been manufactured in the USA by converting standard semi-automatic pistols to full-auto. The process is relatively simple as all that is required is to fill in the space that normally allows the trigger lever to pivot down out of contact with the slide. Therefore, when the slide moves to the rear the trigger lever remains in contact with the slide; thus when the slide moves forward again the trigger lever will contact the slide, pivoting the lever and allowing the pistol to keep firing as long as the trigger is depressed.

A pair of Hard Times Armory select-fire High-Powers; the one at top has the selector set for semi-automatic fire and the one at bottom has the selector set for full-auto fire. (Author's Collection)

based on the Beretta 92; also in use are the Glock 17 and HK USP), Thailand (GP 35; other pistols include the HK USP, HS2000, CZ 75, Beretta 92 and M1951 and FN Five-seveN), Turkey (reported limited High-Power use by the General Directorate of Security, unknown origin; current primary military pistol is the Yavuz, a Turkish copy of the Beretta 92; also in use the Kılınç 2000, a Turkish copy of the CZ 75), Vietnam (limited number captured during the Vietnam War; other pistols used include captured examples of the M1911A1, but principal weapons include the Tokarev TT-33, Makarov PM and CZ 82).

THE HIGH-POWER IN THE MIDDLE EAST

High-Power variants have been widely used across the Middle East since 1945. Among users of the pistol are Bahrain (FN GP 35), Iran (FN GP 35;

Far less common are select-fire versions of the High-Power, which require a selector that will block or unblock the space that allows the trigger lever to pivot downward. Hard Times Armory, which is no longer in business, produced both full-auto and select-fire versions of the High-Power. The examples that the author has examined and fired are based on Inglis High-Powers, at least in part because if they are the No. 1 version, the pistols may have a shoulder stock mounted to allow better control on full-auto fire.

Although a select-fire High-Power is interesting, for most situations a semi-automatic High-Power pistol fired quickly will be just as effective or even more so as it will be easier to control.

The author firing the select-fire High-Power on full-auto; note the empty cases ejecting from the pistol. (Author's Collection)

the primary pistol in current use is the PC-9 ZOAF, a locally produced version of the SIG Sauer P226), Iraq, Israel (assorted FN GP 35 pistols were captured at various times or purchased; also some were reportedly locally produced or assembled; a wide array of handguns have seen usage, with the domestically produced Jericho 941 being standard issue; the Glock 17 and Glock 19 have seen use with Israeli special-operations forces), Jordan (FN GP 35; among pistols currently used are the locally produced Viper and Caracal F; also used by special-operations forces and others are the SIG Sauer P226, Glock 17, Glock 19, HK USP and Beretta 92F), Kuwait (FN GP 35; more recently the Beretta 92), Lebanon, Oman (FN GP 35; the SIG Sauer P226 is also in use), Saudi Arabia (FN GP 35; the SIG Sauer P226 and Glock are currently in use), Syria (the FN GP 35 alongside the Makarov PM and Tokarev TT-33) and the United Arab Emirates (FN GP 35; the primary current-issue pistol is the domestically produced Caracal; also in use is the SIG Sauer P228).

THE HIGH-POWER IN IRAQI SERVICE

Iraqi forces have carried the High-Power alongside the CZ 75, Beretta M1951 and Makarov PM; at the time of writing, Glock 19 pistols are in general use. Although Iraq purchased High-Powers directly from FN, High-Powers made by the Hungarian company Fegyver- és Gépgyártó Részvénytársaság (FÉG: Arms and Machine Manufacturing Company) were also acquired. Reportedly, Saddam Hussein wanted to order FN-made pistols but had problems with the order, possibly because of an arms embargo. However, an enterprising individual purchased a run of FÉG MOD PJK-9HP pistols at far less than the FN version would have cost and had them marked as FN pistols. These were then sold on to the Iraqis. This transaction cheated the Iraqis of substantial amounts of

This engraved High-Power was presented by the Saudi Royal Family to Iraqi General Hussein Kamel. (Courtesy of Rock Island Auction Company)

A close-up of the engraved name of General Hussein Kamel on his presentation pistol. (Courtesy of Rock Island Auction Company)

money as an FN High-Power sold for considerably more than a Hungarian one.

The High-Power was very popular with high-ranking members of the Iraqi ruling class. Saddam Hussein was known to carry a High-Power, reportedly FN-made, that he often fired in the air during rallies to stir up his supporters. Another intricately engraved High-Power was presented by the Saudi Royal Family to General Hussein Kamel, Saddam Hussein's son-in-law. In January 1996, Kamel was killed by members of his own family, and the pistol eventually ended up with a former CIA officer.

One of the 'fake' FN High-Powers sold to Iraq. (Author's Collection)

October 1995: A jubilant Iraqi fires what appears to be one of the 'fake' FN High-Powers sold to Iraq while holding a photo of Saddam Hussein. (Barry Iverson/The LIFE Images Collection via Getty Images)

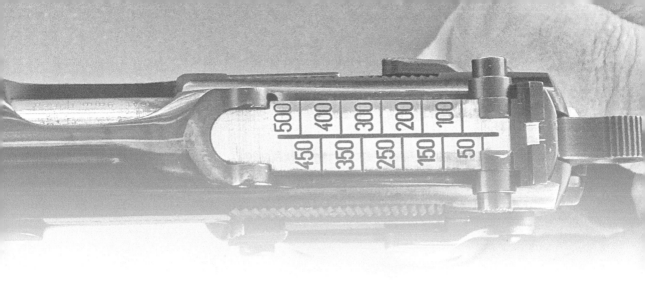

IMPACT
An influential handgun

THE HIGH-POWER AND ITS COMPETITORS

When the High-Power was introduced in 1935, most of the world's armies were in a transitional period between revolvers and semi-automatic pistols. Some had adopted semi-automatic pistols early and were still using models dating from early in the 20th century. The two major competitors for the High-Power at its introduction were the German P 08 Luger and the US Colt M1911. The Luger, especially, was widely employed by countries in various parts of the world, while the M1911 was used by the USA and a few other countries.

The Luger is, of course, one of the classic semi-automatic pistol designs of all time, but by the dawn of World War II it had become outdated. One of the great advantages of the High-Power over the Luger and the Colt M1911 was its simplicity in disassembly for maintenance. Both the Luger and M1911 required far more steps for disassembly and also had more parts that could become lost in the field. When compared to the Luger, the High-Power was also more reliable, the Luger being more dependent upon high-quality ammunition, though ammunition quality control is a factor in the reliability of all semi-automatic pistols. The M1911 was known for its reliability.

Both the High-Power and Luger chambered the 9×19mm cartridge, while the M1911 chambered the .45 ACP cartridge. With full-metal-jacketed military ammunition, the .45 ACP cartridge had the edge in stopping power. One of the great advantages of the High-Power was its magazine capacity of 13, compared to seven for the M1911 and eight for the Luger. Despite that high magazine capacity, the High-Power's grip was very comfortable for many users and allowed instinctive use. However, other users believe that the Luger's grip offers one of the most natural pointings of any pistol.

All three pistols had thumb safeties, while the M1911 also had a grip safety. Arguably, the grip safety made the M1911 safer if the pistol slipped from the hand, though some users found that they had trouble depressing the grip safety properly to allow firing of the pistol. Sights on all three pistols were rudimentary.

Two other 9×19mm pistols introduced around the same time as the High-Power are worthy of comparison: the Polish wz. 35 Vis, known in the English-speaking world as the Radom and also making its debut in 1935, and the German P 38, introduced in 1938 as a replacement for the Luger.

The Radom was never really a competitor with the High-Power in terms of sales, as it was produced in Poland only for the Polish Army and for German armed forces during the occupation of Poland from September 1939 to May 1945. The Radom was actually based on the same Browning system used in the High-Power and was a traditional, single-action 9×19mm semi-automatic pistol with a single-column magazine. One interesting feature that would appear on many later designs was the incorporation of a de-cocking lever on the slide that cammed the firing pin up into the slide to allow the hammer to be safely dropped when the chamber was loaded. This feature was reportedly incorporated so that Polish Army cavalrymen could de-cock their pistols while controlling their horses. The Radom also incorporated a thumb safety and a grip safety.

The P 38, on the other hand, was an innovative pistol that would remain in service into the 21st century. Although there had been double-action pistols in the past, the P 38 was a true 9×19mm military pistol that incorporated the double-action option for the first shot, with subsequent rounds capable of being fired single action. A de-cocking lever on the slide safely dropped the hammer on a loaded chamber. The P 38 employed a single-column magazine holding eight rounds. Adopted by the German armed forces as a replacement for the Luger, the P 38 was reliable and more 'soldier proof' in that to carry the pistol ready for action, it was not necessary to load the chamber and carry the pistol with the hammer cocked and safety on. The High-Power still had the advantage of a very comfortable grip and higher magazine capacity, but the double-action mechanism made the P 38 a popular choice for police and military units. Generally, the P 38's trigger pull on single action is not as good as that of the High-Power either. Though not adopted as widely as the High-Power, at least 30 countries used the P 38 or the post-war P1 version.

The P 38's double action foreshadowed that of many of the High-Power's post-World War II competitors. US Army Service Pistol trials carried out in 1954 resulted in the development of a double-action 9×19mm pistol by Smith & Wesson – the Model 39 – which showed the influence of the P 38 in features such as the slide-mounted de-cocking lever. The Model 39 did not use the exposed barrel of the P 38, however, instead having the slide encase the barrel. Its magazine-release button was located to the rear of the trigger guard as on the High-Power and the Colt M1911. The Model 39 was not widely adopted by US armed forces, though some were purchased for issue to US Air Force general officers and for naval aviators. As the first US-produced double-action 9×19mm pistol, however, the Model 39 was a trailblazing effort.

THE HIGH-POWER'S DESIGN INFLUENCE

Although the High-Power marks the final step in the evolution of John Browning's pistol design that occurred within his lifetime, the influence of the Browning's short-recoil system for semi-automatic pistols remains evident in many contemporary pistol designs. Arguably, though, an equally important influence of the High-Power has been in the proliferation of pistol designs with large magazine capacities. Actually, Browning himself had been influenced by the double-column magazine of the .380 Savage M1907 pistol, but Browning's genius had been to adapt it to a 9×19mm military pistol.

One of the earliest designs after the introduction of the GP 35 to incorporate a high-capacity magazine was the SIG SP44/16, which had a 16-round magazine. The SP44/16 was deemed to have a grip too thick for many hands, however. As a result, the pistol that was favoured was the SIG SP47/8 with an eight-round magazine. This design became renowned as the Swiss military P49 and its commercial version, the P210.

Designed by France's Manufacture d'armes de Bayonne (MAB), the 9×19mm PA15 pistol had a 15-round magazine. A delayed-blowback design introduced in 1966, the PA15 achieved some commercial success and limited military use, mostly by African countries within the French sphere of influence. The PA15 was heavy (1.37kg loaded) and not well balanced, and thus provided little competition to the High-Power, one of the most natural pointing pistols available.

The high magazine capacity of the High-Power and the double-action mechanism of the P 38 were combined by Smith & Wesson in the Model 59, which used the same double-action mechanism as the Model 39. Introduced in 1971, the Model 59 offered a 14-round magazine

The post-war Czech CZ 75 was based to a large extent on the High-Power, though it incorporated a double-action trigger. However, it could also be used as a single-action handgun with a thumb safety. (Author's Collection)

capacity and double action for the first shot, but it was also ungainly when compared to the High-Power. The Model 59 did not incorporate a comfortable grip as did the High-Power and its trigger pull was unimpressive; nor did it really offer much competition to the High-Power for military sales. Improved versions, such as the M459 and M5906, would achieve substantial law-enforcement and some military sales, however.

Introduced in 1975, the Czech CZ 75 was developed primarily for export as it was chambered for the 9×19mm cartridge, while the standard Warsaw Pact round was the 9×18mm Makarov cartridge. The CZ 75 shows extensive influence by the High-Power but with some improvements. Its double-column magazine holds 15 rounds as compared to 13 rounds for the High-Power. Most important in a pistol taking a high-capacity magazine, the CZ 75 retains the ergonomic, natural pointing grip of the High-Power. The CZ 75 also incorporates a double-action system, but one with a safety lever that allows the pistol to be carried with a round chambered, the hammer cocked and the safety on ('cocked and locked'). The only disadvantage of the system is that there is no de-cocker, thus requiring that the hammer be manually lowered with the chamber loaded if intending to fire the first round double action. Many countries adopted the CZ 75 for military or police usage, including the Czech Republic and Slovakia after the demise of the Warsaw Pact. At least 20 countries produced copies of the CZ 75. The author has used the CZ 75 extensively and rates it highly as a combat pistol that retains many of the advantages of the High-Power while offering double-action capability.

By the 1980s, numerous pistols with high-capacity magazines were available, though most were double-action designs. An exception was the P14-45 pistol produced by the Canadian firm Para-Ordnance, this being a single-action double-column semi-automatic chambered for the .45 ACP cartridge. As might be imagined, the P14-45's grip was quite thick.

Offering high magazine capacity, the double-action Smith & Wesson Model 59 combined appealing features of the Browning High-Power and Walther P 38 and proved highly successful. This is the M5946 version adopted by the Royal Canadian Mounted Police. (Author's Collection)

LICENSED AND UNLICENSED MANUFACTURERS OF THE HIGH-POWER

Various countries have manufactured copies of the High-Power, some exact and some with alterations. One of the best-known examples licensed by FN is the Argentinian FM model produced by Fábrica Militar de Armas Portátiles (FMAP) in Rosario. The version produced for military sales is of FN type *c*.1965, with plastic grips and a phosphate finish (Stevens 1984: 260). FM High-Power pistols imported into the US are normally designated the MILITAR M90. While early FM pistols resembled 1960s-era FN pistols, after FN introduced the improved Mk II High-Power, the FM eventually incorporated some of the improvements, including high-visibility sights, a polished feed ramp for the use of hollow-point ammunition, and an ambidextrous safety. For enhanced safety, later FMs also incorporated a positive firing-pin safety. Based on the author's experience, these later FM pistols also have a better trigger pull than that normally encountered on High-Power pistols. Finish is black phosphate. Also imported into the USA have been .22 units for the FM to allow inexpensive training with the pistol. FMAP has marketed a shortened version of the High-Power as the 'Detective Model'.

India produces a copy of the High-Power that is reportedly licensed, though it is actually a copy of the Inglis No. 2 Mk 1* High-Power rather than the FN version. Designated the Pistol Auto 9mm 1A, it is manufactured by the Rifle Factory Ishapore. Law offers the theory that these copies of the Inglis No. 2 Mk 1* may be based on some of the 4,000 Inglis-built pistols shipped to India for the Chinese that went missing (Law 2001: 262). However, as the 1A is a copy of the Inglis No. 2 Mk 1*, it is more likely to have been based on Inglis No. 2 Mk 1* pistols left behind by British troops in India.

Another licensed copy of the High-Power was produced by Defence Industries Corporation of Nigeria. The author has not had a chance to examine a Nigerian High-Power, but presumably it would be similar to the standard FN model of the 1960s.

Among unlicensed copies of the High-Power is the Pindad produced in Indonesia and used by the Indonesian Army. Slide markings were 'PABRIK SENDJATA RINGAN PINDAD'. According to Stevens, at least 30,000 Pindad High-Powers were produced (Stevens 1984: 264). Based on their scarcity in the USA, it appears that the Pindad High-Power was never exported.

The most interesting unlicensed version of the High-Power is that produced by Fegyver- és Gépgyártó Részvénytársaság (FÉG: Arms and Machine Manufacturing Company) in Hungary. This pistol is designated the FÉG MOD PJK-9HP, though it has also been designated the P9M. Some FÉG High-Powers were sold under the Mauser name. Although early FÉG PJK High-Powers closely resemble the FN product, there are various later versions that do not. The FP9, for example, has a rib atop the slide and the P9R has a double-action mechanism of Smith & Wesson type.

The Bulgarian Arcus is another pistol derived from the High-Power. While part of the Warsaw Pact (1955–91), Bulgaria produced the Makarov pistol for internal law-enforcement and military usage. Once the Cold War ended and Bulgaria was free to compete on the open market, however, Arcus Company of Lyaskovets, Bulgaria, began producing a High-Power copy designated the Arcus 94. Low-cost labour has made the Arcus 94 very competitive in the US market for an inexpensive yet reliable combat pistol.

The Arcus 94 incorporates many standard FN High-Power features, including a magazine safety, but other features are more akin to the Mk II High-Power with an ambidextrous safety and high-visibility, low-profile combat sights. Arcus claims that standard Browning High-Power

The Hungarian FÉG MOD PJK-9HP version of the High-Power. Many parts of this unlicensed copy reportedly interchange with those produced by FN. As is evident here, the FÉG pistol resembles the FN product to such an extent that one can understand how Saddam Hussein's regime fell victim to the scam discussed on pages 64 and 65. (Author's Collection)

magazines may be used in the Arcus 94. One noteworthy feature is the finger-grooved grips on some pistols, a feature the author, a fan of the traditional High-Power grip, does not like. A grip closer to the traditional High-Power grip is also available.

Arcus also makes a double-action pistol, the Arcus 98, also derived from the High-Power. The Arcus 98 shows the influence of the Czech CZ 75 as well, however, in that it offers the option of carrying the pistol 'cocked and locked'. The Arcus 98 is reportedly standard issue with the Bulgarian military and police.

REPLACING THE HIGH-POWER

Entering the scene in 1975, the same year as the CZ 75, the Beretta 92 was a DA/SA design that took a 15-round magazine. Initially, the Beretta 92 used a frame-mounted thumb safety and a bottom magazine release. On the Beretta 92S, however, the thumb safety was replaced with a slide-mounted de-cocker/safety. For US military trials, a firing-pin block, three-dot sights, ambidextrous de-cocker/safety levers, and magazine-release button behind the trigger guard were added for the 92S-1 version, which won the trials and with a few additional modifications was adopted as the M9 pistol.

The M9 proved to be more user-friendly than the M1911 pistol and also easier to shoot for smaller users, as it was chambered for the 9×19mm cartridge instead of the .45 ACP round. Its DA/SA mechanism also made it a quicker pistol to bring into action when carried with a round in the chamber and the hammer down. Its adoption by US armed forces made it a popular choice for other armed forces wanting to upgrade to a modern 'Wonder Nine' (a term sometimes used for the early double-action, high-capacity pistols). In some cases countries adopted a less expensive copy such as the Taurus PT-92. The M9 served as the principal US military handgun for more than 30 years, only having been replaced by the SIG Sauer M17 in 2017. Unlike many other pistols taking a high-capacity magazine, the Beretta 92 has a relatively comfortable grip, though not quite as good as that of the High-Power in the author's opinion. Its sights are better than those of the High-Power and, of course, it can be carried safely yet ready for a quick first shot using a double-action trigger pull. Nevertheless, only a few countries using the High-Power chose to replace it with the Beretta 92/M9.

Another pistol that fared well in the US military pistol trials was the SIG Sauer P226. SIG Sauer had developed a new service pistol for the Swiss Army that was adopted as the P75. This 9×19mm pistol was a high-quality double-action design but with a single-column magazine. For the XM9 Service Pistol Trials held to choose a new US service pistol, the P226 high-capacity pistol was developed based on the P220, the commercial designation for the P75. Unlike the Beretta 92, the P226 employs a de-cocking lever on the frame that automatically drops the hammer safely and then returns to the off position so the pistol is ready for a first-round double-action shot. Its standard magazine holds 15 rounds, though longer 20-round magazines are available for special usage. The P226 completed the US trials successfully along with the Beretta 92, but as the Beretta was cheaper it was adopted. The US Navy SEALs adopted the P226, however, as the Mk 25. The SAS and some other British military units also adopted the P226 or its compact version, the P228, as the L105A1 and L107A1 respectively.

Advantages of the P226 vis-à-vis the High-Power are its DA/SA mechanism, its high-capacity magazine and its accuracy. SIG Sauer pistols have a reputation for reliability and accuracy, and the P226 is no exception. The primary disadvantage of the P226 as a general-issue military pistol is that its grip is fat, making it difficult for some users with small hands to fire it effectively. Although the P226 has made some inroads among countries formerly using the High-Power, it has primarily been adopted for use by special-forces units rather than for general issue.

The pistol that would supplant the High-Power in military service with a substantial number of countries was the Glock. First introduced in 1982, the Glock was viewed with suspicion as a 'plastic pistol'. Its revolutionary design employed a polymer frame with an operating system that is actually adapted from the High-Power. The original Glock, which is still the most widely used model among military and police units, is the Glock 17. Among the Glock's advantages are its light weight, fewer parts than many other pistols, 17-round magazine capacity, and the 'Safe-Action' trigger system that renders the pistol safe until the trigger is pulled, thus no thumb safeties must be released. There is a lever safety located within the trigger.

Two of the great selling points for the Glock are its low price and its durability (there are Glock pistols used at training facilities that have fired 500,000-plus rounds). The Glock is also light in weight and is

CUSTOMIZING THE HIGH-POWER

The High-Power has been used as a combat pistol for so long that its strengths and shortcomings are well known by its users. In its later High-Powers such as the Mk II, FN addressed some of the deficiencies, but many users still did not find High-Power pistols available from FN or Browning to be optimized for close combat. As a result, in the USA and in some other countries where the High-Power was widely used, custom gunsmiths offered upgrades.

The author has carried and used the High-Power for almost 50 years and has fired many of the enhanced High-Powers produced by custom gunsmiths. To illustrate the operations normally performed as part of the customizing process, two custom High-Powers he uses are described here.

The first was built by ROBAR Guns of Phoenix, Arizona, and involved the following modifications: Novak front and Lo-Mount rear sights installed; front and back straps stippled; beavertail fabricated; BAR STO barrel installed; feed ramp polished; cylinder and slide High-Power hammer installed; trigger job performed; cylinder and slide ambidextrous safety installed; pistol completely de-burred; magazine safety de-activated, allowing the empty magazine to drop free; magazine well bevelled; pistol given a Roguard finish, with NP3 on the internals; Spegel slim High-Power grips installed.

The author's second custom High-Power was built by Jim Garthwaite of Watsontown, Pennsylvania, and incorporates the

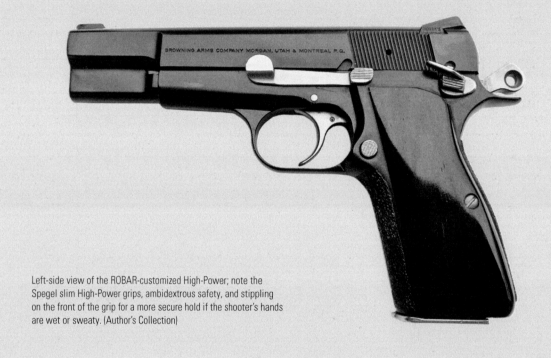

Left-side view of the ROBAR-customized High-Power; note the Spegel slim High-Power grips, ambidextrous safety, and stippling on the front of the grip for a more secure hold if the shooter's hands are wet or sweaty. (Author's Collection)

ready for immediate engagement upon drawing it. The author has owned, carried and fired various models of the Glock and is cognizant of its strong points. When compared to the High-Power, however, there are some disadvantages. First, the author finds the High-Power's grip to be more comfortable, though the Glock's grip has been made more ergonomic in recent years, including allowing the size of the grip to be adjusted through the use of a modular back-strap system. Because of the lack of an external safety that must be manipulated prior to firing the Glock, there have been a substantial number of negligent discharges with the pistol. A strict training regimen and a proper holster are a necessity if the Glock is to be safely used as a military or law-enforcement pistol. Countering the safety issue is the fact that the Glock may be following features: Heinie Slant Pro rear fixed sight installed; front sight with Garthwaite Gold Bead insert installed; front and back straps stippled; magazine well bevelled; Garthwaite custom thumb safety (non-ambidextrous) installed; complete trigger job performed; BAR STO barrel installed; Wolff recoil and firing-pin springs installed; rear of slide chequered; complete pistol Teflon-coated; Spegel slim High-Power grips installed.

This custom work is designed to increase accuracy, reliability, durability and ergonomics. Accuracy enhancements are achieved through better sights, better trigger pull and the BAR STO barrels. Operations such as polishing the feed ramp and de-burring the pistol improve the reliability of feeding hollow-point and other types of ammunition. While installation of high-quality springs ensures that the pistol will function more reliably, the special finishes help the pistols to hold up to hard use in adverse conditions. Stippling or otherwise treating the front and back strap allows a surer grip when the hand is wet. Among features that enhance ergonomics or allow the pistol to be used more quickly in combat are a bevelled magazine well for faster magazine changes and an ambidextrous or otherwise altered safety. Removing the magazine safety allows a magazine to drop free for a faster change, but also aids in enhancing the trigger pull. Spegel High-Power grips are slimmer and allow an even more comfortable grip when shooting the High-Power, especially when engaging multiple targets.

Right-side view of the Garthwaite-customized High-Power showing the BAR STO barrel for greater accuracy; note also the chequered Spegel grips of the type used by the FBI Hostage Rescue Team. (Author's Collection)

carried ready for immediate engagement of an enemy; one reason the British Army adopted it for issue in Afghanistan where the chance of an attack by Taliban fighters was always present. Most armies that issued (or issue) the High-Power generally trained their troops to carry it without a round in the chamber: Condition Three. As a result, prior to engagement, it was necessary to rack the slide, thus eating time that could possibly be life-saving.

Over the last decade, numerous countries have replaced the High-Power with the Glock, and it seems likely that this trend will continue. It should be noted, however, that at least some of those countries that have adopted the Glock continue to have troops carry it in the same Condition Three (without a round in the chamber) as the High-Power!

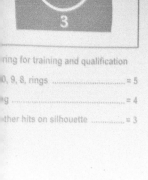

CONCLUSION

The High-Power pistol was John Browning's final design and is considered by many to be his best. The FN FAL battle rifle has been called 'The Right Arm of the Free World' because so many countries adopted it as their service rifle. To take the analogy further: the FN High-Power pistol was adopted by so many countries that it could be termed 'The Right Hand of the Free World'. From its introduction in 1935 until the beginning of the 21st century, the High-Power offered reliability, high magazine capacity, good ergonomics and accuracy; but the availability of double-action, high-capacity autoloaders with lightweight frames and more recently of polymer-framed, striker-fired pistols with high magazine capacity has caused the High-Power to be replaced in the armouries of many countries that used it for decades. Recently, FNH discontinued production of the High-Power after 83 years. Many of those who have used the High-Power, including the author, were saddened by its demise. Estimates of total production vary, but the number is approaching two million or more. In the USA and other countries with large civilian ownership of handguns, the High-Power remains a sought-after pistol for self-defence and collecting.

Because so many countries have used the High-Power, collectors have myriad variations to seek. Some High-Powers sport the crests of countries or military or police units; some have special features. Collectors also try to obtain High-Powers embodying the design and engineering changes from the earliest FN pistols for the Belgian Army to the last production runs. Many elite military and law-enforcement units have used the High-Power, from the SAS to the FBI HRT, which lends the pistol a certain cachet. High-Powers have also been used by intelligence agents and other clandestine warriors and have found use in the mercenary wars in Africa. The High-Power has been the choice of dictators such as Saddam Hussein and Muammar Gaddafi. From the battlefields of World War II through to the 'War on Terror', the High-Power has been one of the most prized trophies. US GIs traditionally coveted captured High-Powers because they took readily available 9×19mm ammunition and held a lot of rounds. While at war it was a GI's companion that could be kept close at hand and when they returned home it was a trophy that reminded them of their time in combat.

The High-Power feels and looks like a combat pistol. Just having one on the hip or in the hand gives a sense of being more prepared to face danger. Among lists of the most important handguns of all times, the High-Power normally is among the Top Ten – even higher among the most important military pistols.

Determining the most influential semi-automatic pistol in history is difficult, as many pistols have influenced some aspect of the self-loader's design. Early designs such as the Borchardt C93, Mauser C96, Bergmann 1896, Schwarzlose 1898 and Luger 1900 all contributed to later designs. John Browning's designs, especially the M1911, influenced later military pistols. Although the double-action semi-automatic pistol can trace its lineage back to the 'Little Tom' pistol, it was the Walther P 38 that popularized the double-action mechanism for a military service pistol. Likewise, there were pistols with double-column magazines before the High-Power, but it was the High-Power that made the high-capacity pistol a viable military choice. Other features that were incorporated into the High-Power such as the magazine safety and the simplified takedown have been used on other semi-automatic pistols subsequently.

A more direct influence of the High-Power has been on the number of copies that have been made as well as the various pistols, such as the CZ 75, that show the marked influence of the High-Power in their design. Despite all of the efforts to make modern semi-automatic pistols more ergonomic by offering interchangeable grips and back straps, in the present author's view the High-Power's grip remains one of the most comfortable ever on a pistol, especially a high-capacity one.

The question remains: why did FNH discontinue the High-Power? The answer is probably multifaceted. Many of the countries that have used the High-Power as their standard military pistol for decades have decided to replace it with one of the more 'modern' designs from Glock, SIG Sauer or Heckler & Koch. Civilian customers in those countries where they could purchase a High-Power, principally the USA, have also become enamoured of the high-capacity, double-action, polymer-framed pistols. Most fans of the High-Power are older and probably already own one or more of the pistols. Younger shooters want Glocks or other 'black pistols'. The US civilian pistol market is driven today by the large number of concealed-weapons licensees, who want 9×19mm pistols that are more compact and concealable than the High-Power. For those who do still want to purchase a High-Power there are surplus law-enforcement examples that may be imported into the USA for sale. There are also clones from countries that have produced licensed and unlicensed copies of the High-Power.

FNH has focused on its more recent pistol designs, including the FNX, FNS, FN509 and FN Five-seveN, while production of another legendary FN weapon, the FAL battle rifle, has also been discontinued. Instead, the company produces the FN15 (the FN version of the AR-15/M16) and the FN SCAR rifles.

BIBLIOGRAPHY

Campbell, Dave (2017). 'A Look Back at the Browning High-Power Pistol', https://www.americanrifleman.org/articles/2017/10/24/a-look-back-at-the-browning-high-power-pistol/

Campbell, R.K. (2012a). 'The Browning High Power', *Small Arms Review*, http://www.smallarmsreview.com/display.article.cfm?idarticles=383

Campbell, R.K. (2012b). 'The Inglis High Power Pistol', *Small Arms Review*, http://www.smallarmsreview.com/display.article.cfm?idarticles=1503

Coulson, Danny (1999). *No Errors: Inside the FBI's Secret Counter-Terror Force*. New York, NY: Pocket Books.

Dabbs, Will (2018). 'The Browning HI Power: The Superlative WWII Combat Handgun that Played Both Sides', *Guns America Digest*, https://www.gunsamerica.com/digest/browning-hi-power/

Eger, Chris (2018). 'Iconic Browning Hi-Power Ends Production After More than 80 Years', Guns.com, https://www.guns.com/news/2018/02/08/iconic-browning-hi-power-ends-production-after-more-than-80-years

Ezell, Edward (1981). *Handguns of the World: Military Revolvers and Self-Loaders from 1870 to 1945*. Harrisburg, PA: Stackpole Books.

Ezell, Edward (1988). *Small Arms Today*. 2nd Edition. Harrisburg, PA: Stackpole Books.

Francotte, Auguste, et al. (2008). *Ars Mechanica: The Ultimate FN Book*. Liège: Herstal Group.

Gander, Terry (1998). *Germany's Infantry Weapons 1939–45*. Ramsbury: Crowood.

Huard, Paul Richard (2014). 'Everybody Loved Their Browning Hi-Powers Back in the Day', War is Boring, https://warisboring.com/everybody-loved-their-browning-hi-powers-back-in-the-day/

jaypee (2017). 'Photographic Glossary of High Power Discussion Terms', Highpowercollectors, http://highpowercollectors.proboards.com/thread/170/photographic-glossary-power-discussion-terms

Keightley, Richard (2014). *Deter, Suppress, Extract! Royal Military Police Close Protection: The Authorized History*. Solihull: Helion.

Law, Clive (2001). *Inglis Diamond: The Canadian High-Power Pistol*. Cobourg: Collector Grade Publications.

Long, Tony (2016). *Lethal Force: My Life as the Met's Most Controversial Marksman*. London: Ebury.

Page, Lewis (2013). 'British Armed Forces to Get First New Pistol Since World War II', *The Register*, 11 January 2013 https://www.theregister.co.uk/2013/01/11/browning_9mm_finally_replaced/

Plaster, John (2016). 'SOG's Most Exclusive Memorabilia: Silver Pistol', available at https://ultimatesniper.com/wp-content/uploads/2016/06/SOGS-Most-Exclusive-Memorabilia-Silver-Pistol.pdf

Popenker, Maxim (no date). 'FN Browning HP-DA BDA-9', Modern Firearms, http://modernfirearms.net/en/handguns/handguns-en/belgium-semi-automatic-pistols/fn-browning-hp-da-bda9-eng/

Pugliese, David (2017). 'Canadian Forces looking to replace Second World War-era pistols but it could take another 10 years', *National Post*, https://nationalpost.com/news/canada/canadian-forces-looking-to-replace-second-world-war-era-pistols-but-it-could-take-another-10-years

Rennie, James (1996). *The Operators: On the Streets with 14th Intelligence Company*. London: Century.

Stevens, R. Blake (1984). *The Browning High-Power Automatic Pistol*. Toronto: Collector Grade Publications.

Thompson, Leroy (2011). *The Colt 1911 Pistol*. Weapon 9. Oxford: Osprey Publishing.

Vanderlinden, Anthony (2013). *FN Browning Pistols: Side-Arms That Shaped World History*. Greensboro, NC: Wet Dog Publications.

Vanderlinden, Anthony (2015a). '5 Little-Known Facts About the FN Browning High-Power', *American Rifleman*, https://www.americanrifleman.org/articles/2015/12/2/5-little-known-facts-about-the-fn-browning-high-power/

Vanderlinden, Anthony (2015b). '80 Years of the Belgian High Power', *American Rifleman*, https://www.americanrifleman.org/articles/2015/9/23/80-years-of-the-belgian-high-power/

Various (1995). 'Browning .40 S&W Hi-Power', Dope Bag, *American Rifleman*, July 1995, pp. 48–49. Available at http://www.nramuseum.org/media/363967/Jul%2095.pdf

Various (2005). 'Finnish FN P35s (Finnish contract HiPowers)', The High Road, https://www.thehighroad.org/index.php?threads/finnish-fn-p35s-finnish-contract-hipowers.125847/

Various (2009). 'SAS Modifications to the Basic Hi Power', Handguns & Ammunition, https://www.handgunsandammunition.com/hi-power-forum/7270-sas-modifications-basic-hi-power.html

Various (2012). 'Browning Hi-Power in .30 Luger', 1911forum.com, https://forums.1911forum.com/showthread.php?t=484707

Various (2016). 'Assembled in Portugal: When did it start and which kinds of HPs?' 1911forum.com, https://forums.1911forum.com/showthread.php?t=630009

Waldren, Michael J. (2007). *Armed Police: The Police Use of Firearms since 1945*. Stroud: Sutton Publishing.

Whittington, Maj. Robert D. (1976). *German Pistols and Holsters 1934/1945: Military–Police, NSDAP*. Highland Park, NJ: The Gun Room Press.

Wilson, R.K. & Hogg, Ian V. (1975). *Textbook of Automatic Pistols*. London: Arms & Armour Press.

INDEX